"SIDE-SPLITTING, MEGABYTE-SIZE HUMOR."
—*St. Petersburg Times*

"Something funny is going on in Cyberspace, and dbarry@techgeek.com is just the guy to tell us about it."
—*Atlanta Journal & Constitution*

"The latest in Barry's bestselling string of often riotously funny humor books. It proves that even geeks can get hopelessly lost in cyberspace, and he gives the rest of us a roadmap.
—*The Cleveland Plain Dealer*

"If you don't love it . . . you're in a distinct minority."
—*Booklist*

"Pointed and funny . . . A natural topic for a prize-winning humorist.
—*Kirkus Reviews*

"Nonstop humor . . . Whether you're a computer whiz or a computer nerd, this tongue-in-cheek guide to computing by bestselling humorist Dave Barry has enough byte to keep you entertained."
—*Publishers Weekly*

"Hilariously imaginative."
—*Library Journal*

ALSO BY DAVE BARRY

The Taming of the Screw

Babies and Other Hazards of Sex

Stay Fit and Healthy Until You're Dead

Claw Your Way to the Top

Bad Habits

Dave Barry's Guide to Marriage and/or Sex

Homes and Other Black Holes

Dave Barry's Greatest Hits

Dave Barry Turns 40

Dave Barry's Only Travel Guide You'll Ever Need

Dave Barry Talks Back

Dave Barry Does Japan

Dave Barry Is Not Making This Up

Dave Barry's Complete Guide to Guys

Dave Barry's Gift Guide to End All Gift Guides

Dave Barry's Book of Bad Songs

Dave Barry Is from Mars and Venus

Dave Barry Turns 50

Big Trouble

Dave Barry Is Not Taking This Sitting Down

Dave Barry Hits Below the Beltway

Dave Barry in
CYBERSPACE

DAVE BARRY

Fawcett Books
New York

A Fawcett Book
Published by The Ballantine Publishing Group

Copyright © 1996 by Dave Barry

All rights reserved under International and Pan-American
Copyright Conventions. Published in the United States by
Ballantine Books, a division of Random House, Inc., New York,
and simultaneously in Canada by Random House of Canada
Limited, Toronto.

Fawcett and colophon are trademarks of Random House, Inc.

www.ballantinebooks.com

Library of Congress Catalog Card Number: 97-90891

ISBN: 0-449-91230-2

This edition published by arrangement with Crown Publishers, Inc.

Book design by Susan Hood

Cover photo by Bill Wax

Manufactured in the United States of America

First Ballantine Books Edition: October 1997

10 9 8 7 6 5

For Hoobert and MsPtato
With special thanks to Crow

CONTENTS

Introduction   1

1: A Brief History of Computing from   15
   Cave Walls to Windows 95
   Not That This Is Necessarily Progress

2: How Computers Work   31

3: How to Buy and Set Up a Computer   39
   Step One: Get Valium

4: Becoming Computer Literate   53
   Or: Words for Nerds

5: Comdex   59
   Nerdstock in the Desert
   Or: Bill Gates Is Elvis

6: Software   79
   Making Your Computer Come Alive So It
     Can Attack You

7: How to Install Software   97
   A 12-Step Program

8: Word Processing   101
   How to Press an Enormous Number of Keys
      Without Ever Actually Writing Anything
   Or: If God Had Wanted Us to Be Concise, He
      Wouldn't Have Given Us So Many Fonts

9: The Internet   121
   Transforming Society and Shaping the Future,
      Through Chat
   Or: Watch What You Write, Mr. Chuckletrousers
   Or: Why Suck Is OK, Blow Is Not
   Plus: Danger! Sushi Tapeworms!

10: Using Internet "Shorthand"   141
   How You Can Be Just as Original as Everybody Else

11: Selected Web Sites   149
   At Last: Proof That Civilization Is Doomed

12: MsPtato and RayAdverb   169
   A Story of Love On-line

13: Conclusion   203
   The Future of the Computer Revolution
   Or: Fun with Mister Johnson

14: Reprise   211
   MsPtato and RayAdverb

INTRODUCTION

You need to know right off the bat that I'm a total computer geek. I am *pathetic*. You've seen all those computer magazines with names like *Data Dweeb* and cover headlines like:

INSIDE:
EXPLICIT COLOR PHOTOGRAPHS
OF BIG HARD DRIVES!

or:

WAX YOUR MODEM FOR IMPROVED SPEED!

No doubt you've asked yourself, "What kind of no-life loser actually *reads* these magazines?"

I do! All the time! I read them in bed! I look at the pictures of new computer systems and become moderately aroused and say things like "Whoa! Check out the 6X SCSI-2 CD-ROM drive on THAT baby!"

I'm always on the lookout for a new computer to replace my current one when it becomes obsolete, which usually happens before I can get it all the way out of the box. I am not proud of this, but I have owned more than twenty computers,[1] dating back to the early 1980s, when I got one of the first primitive Radio Shack models, which looked like a mutant toaster oven that had been exposed to atomic radiation and developed a keyboard.

This computer had virtually no practical use other than to consume electricity. You know how modern personal computers contain a microchip "brain" that, despite being no larger than a Chiclet, can perform millions of mathematical calculations per second? Well, I don't think my Radio Shack computer had one of those. I think there might have been an actual Chiclet in there, calling the shots. Because this frankly was not a gifted computer. I would not have put my money on this computer in a head-to-head IQ test against a doorknob.

I had two programs for my Radio Shack: a word processor and a game where you were a spaceship commander, trying to destroy invading alien spaceships. In terms of enhancing my personal productivity, there was essentially no difference between these two programs. Both were very difficult to get working; both frequently *stopped* working for no apparent reason; and both had insanely obscure instructions that were writ-

1. All of them, fortunately, tax-deductible.

ten neither by nor for human beings. ("To delete a word, you must first enter the Command Mode by pressing the slash key, followed by the percent key, followed by the key with that little squiggly thing, followed by the first five digits of your Social Security number, followed by . . .") It was impossible to use these programs for more than a few minutes without seriously screwing up and losing an important document or (even worse) your spaceship.

But I loved that computer. I spent many happy hours cursing at it. I even learned to program it a little bit. At one point I spent hours writing a simple program that made the computer count. When I ran the program, numbers would appear on the screen in sequence, like this:

1	2	3	4	5	6	7	8	9	10
11	12	13	14	15	16	17	18	19	20
21	22	23	24	25	26	27	28	29	30

. . . and so on, until the Chiclet pooped out. I ran this program over and over. I was proud of myself for developing this innovative way to utilize my data-processing resources to do my counting for me automatically, thereby freeing me to devote my valuable time to the important task of shopping for a new computer.

Of course today I have a far more powerful computer containing numerous important computer things such as "megahertzes" and "megs" of "RAM," and I use it for many vital tasks other than counting. For example, I am writing this book on a computer that is running the hugely popular Windows 95™ operating system, which has revolutionized the software world thanks to its capability of accomplishing the seemingly impossible task of making Bill Gates even richer than he already was.

I love Windows 95™, because first of all, it is so unbelievably complicated that I will never, ever in one trillion years really figure it out; this is an important feature for us computer geeks, who would much rather spend our time diddling with our computers than using them to do something productive. If you don't believe this, pick up a copy of *Byte*[2] magazine sometime and read a column in there by a guy named Jerry Pournelle. Jerry is an author and a famous computer guru, and every month his column has basically the same plot, which is:

1. Jerry tries to make some seemingly simple change to one of his computers, such as connect it to a new printer.

2. Everything goes hideously wrong and the computer completely stops working. Sometimes several of his *other* computers also stop working. Sometimes there are massive power outages all over the West Coast. Poor Larry spends *days* trying to get everything straightened out.

2. This is the real name, I swear.

---

3. Finally, with the help of Customer Service[3] and other computer experts all over the world, Jerry gets his computer working again approximately the way it used to, and he writes several thousand words about it for *Byte*.

I swear it's virtually the same plot, month after month, and yet it's a popular column in a magazine that appeals primarily to knowledgeable computer people. Why? Because Jerry's coming right out and admitting that we knowledgeable computer people primarily use our computers for messing around. Windows 95™, being virtually impossible for a normal human to comprehend, is ideal for this purpose. Also, thanks to its advanced graphical capabilities, Windows 95™ enables you to put the little ™ sign after "Windows 95." In fact, you can put all kinds of little things up there, such as Windows 95®, Windows 95®, Windows 95♠, and of course Windows 95^BILLGATESISAWIENER. (I'll have more to say about dressing up your documents in the chapter on word processing, or "How to Press an Enormous Number of Keys Without Ever Actually Writing Anything.")

And here's another important capability that I have, thanks to the powerful studliness of my computer and Windows 95^*: I can do "multi-tasking," which means I have the ability to run several programs

---

3. Which does not exist outside of Jerry Pournelle columns. More on this later.

at the same time, which means that I can waste time *faster than ever before*.

For example: As I am writing this chapter, I am also running a program called Sim Tower™®©☞, in which you build this simulated building with little simulated elevators, escalators, offices, hotel rooms, etc., and then all these little simulated people come and you have to try to keep them safe and happy. This is not easy. In fact, during the preceding paragraph, when I was trying to solve the complex word-processing problem of how to make the ☠ mark, I received an urgent message informing me that a terrorist had planted a bomb in my building and was demanding that I pay a $1 million ransom. Also I have office workers demanding parking spaces, and a number of my hotel rooms have been invaded by roaches the size of Rush Limbaugh®. Right now I am dealing with these problems, AND writing this informative book about computers, AND using a program called "ABM Commander" to protect several cities from nuclear destruction, AND checking my "e-mail" to get important guidance[4] from my editors. Thanks to the miracle of computers, I am able to accomplish all of these tasks *simultaneously*, in stark contrast to famous authors of the pre-computer era such as Chaucer, who had to stop writing altogether when he wanted to play "ABM Commander."[5]

4. Such as "WHERE THE HELL IS THE COMPUTER BOOK??"
5. Also he had to use a manual typewriter.

My point is that I have learned to use my computer as a productive tool in my everyday life, and you can, too, by applying the many helpful tips and practical techniques that you'll find in this book.[6] Also you can find out how to get on the Internet and make contact with hundreds, even thousands, of people whom you would otherwise never have had anything to do with voluntarily.

But even if you don't use a computer; even if you're just an ordinary human being or member of the legal profession, this book can help you better understand computers—these amazing devices that play such an important role in your life, every minute of every day, from the moment, at 6 A.M. each morning, when you punch your clock radio to make it shut up. Think about it: Inside that clock radio is a miniature computer, an electronic "brain" that, despite being no larger than the reproductive organs of a standard female mosquito, is capable—thanks to the miracle of microcircuitry—of understanding not only basic commands, such as "ON," "OFF," and "ALARM," but also advanced data-processing concepts, such as "SNOOZE."

And that's just the beginning. As clock radios become more intelligent, they'll start to actually anticipate your actions. Even as you read these words, top appliance scientists are working on a prototype clock radio of tomorrow that will have little feet, so that after it sounds the alarm, it can dart around the night-

6. Dream on.

stand, evading your fist. Eventually your clock radio will be so smart that it will figure out, after being punched a few times, that you don't really *want* to wake up at 6 A.M. Instead of sounding the alarm, it will tiptoe quietly out of the room, telephone your workplace, and, mimicking your voice, inform your employer that you're quitting.

A utopian pipe dream, you say? An overly optimistic scenario of life in the high-tech future? I don't think so! Not when we consider the many incredible benefits that we are receiving from computers right now, *today*, in virtually every area of our everyday lives, including:

■ **MEDICINE:** Every day, in every town, there are heartwarming stories like this one: A 53-year-old man suddenly starts experiencing severe chest pains and shortness of breath. An ambulance rushes him to a hospital, where, as his condition rapidly worsens, doctors administer a series of tests, the results of which are instantaneously transmitted via a special fiber-optic telephone cable to a giant medical database computer a thousand miles away. Almost instantaneously an electronic message comes back, informing the doctors that the patient—whom the computer has mistaken for another man, with a similar name who actually died thirty-eight months earlier—has fallen behind in his car payments and should be denied credit at the hospital. The computer then—*without even having to be asked*—disconnects the patient's electrical and phone services and cancels every one of his credit cards. All of this is accomplished in less time than it takes you to burp.

■ **TRANSPORTATION:** When you fly on a commercial airline, you experience the security and comfort of knowing that, even though you may be 35,000 feet in the air, traveling at over 500 miles per hour under conditions of obscured visibility, *not one single passenger on your airplane paid the same fare as any other passenger.* How is this possible? It's possible because the airline industry uses powerful and extremely imaginative fare-inventing computers, which are constantly being improved as the airline industry works toward the day—this will happen in your lifetime—when every single airline passenger pays a different fare from every other passenger *on every other flight in history.* Just recently, in a breakthrough step toward this goal, a Chicago attorney, wishing to fly to Philadelphia, was required to pay two cows and a goat.[7]

■ **COMMUNICATIONS:** Today most of us take it for granted that if we urgently need to reach a person, no matter where that person is in the world, we can simply press a few buttons on a telephone keypad, and within microseconds, thanks to the computerized global satellite telecommunications network, be connected with a microprocessor-controlled, multi-function voice-mail

7. This ticket required a Saturday-night stayover, with a two-sheep penalty for any changes.

machine informing us that the person is not available. But that is only part of the story. Thanks to computers, inanimate objects are now able to contact *us*. I am not referring here to the computers that call us up at exactly dinnertime to ask us prerecorded consumer-survey questions about our views on, for example, laxatives. Nor am I referring to the highly personalized letters that we receive from computers that know our name, and are not about to let us forget it:

*Dear **Mr. Dave Barry:***
*Have you, **Mr. Dave Barry**, ever stopped to think about what would happen to your family—the **Mr. Dave Barry** family—in the tragic event that you, **Mr. Dave Barry**, were to tragically become involved in an accident resulting in the loss of one or more of your, **Mr. Dave Barry's**, key arms and/or legs? Well, we here at Mutual General Admiral Mineral Insurance spend most of our time worrying about exactly this. "We sure hope that **Mr. Dave Barry** has adequate coverage," are our exact words, which is why today we want to offer you, **Mr. Dave** . . .*

No, the specific example of computer communication that I am thinking of here is a widely publicized, absolutely true 1995 news story—you might have read about this—about a woman in Billerica, Massachusetts, who had an 800 telephone number for her home business, on which she received a mysterious telephone call *every 90 minutes*, day and night, for *six months*.

She'd answer the phone, but there was never anybody there, only silence. It was driving her crazy, but she didn't want to disconnect the phone, because she was afraid she'd lose business. Finally she contacted the authorities, who tracked down the source of the calls, which turned out to be—I swear I am not making this up—an unused oil tank in the basement of a home in Potomac, Maryland. This tank was equipped with a computerized device programmed to call a fuel company when the tank was empty, but the fuel company had shut down, and its phone number was reassigned to the Massachusetts woman's business. In other words, thanks to the miracle of computers, this woman was being *harassed by an empty oil tank hundreds of miles away*—a technological achievement that would have been considered impossible just a few short[8] decades ago. In any event, the oil tank is now disconnected, which is good, because otherwise it would probably have wound up registered to vote.[9] And speaking of voting, nowhere are the benefits we receive from computers more flagrant than in the area of:

■ **GOVERNMENT:** Without computers, the government would be unable to function at the level of the effectiveness and efficiency that we have come to expect. This is because the primary function of the government is—and here I am quoting directly from

8. The '60s, for example, only lasted four years. At least that's all I remember.
9. And you *know* it's a Perot supporter.

the U.S. Constitution—"to spew out paper." This can be very time-consuming if you use the old-fashioned method of having human beings sit down and manually think about what each individual piece of paper is actually going to say. This is why today's government uses computers, which are capable of cranking out millions of documents per day without any regard whatsoever for their content, thereby freeing government employees for more important responsibilities, such as not answering their phones. I have here a perfect example of a government computer in action, brought to my attention by Joyce Evans of Larkspur, California, who sent me a copy of a computerized notice that her son, a graduate student, received from the Internal Revenue Service. This notice, entitled "REQUEST FOR TAX PAYMENT," states that her son's tax return showed that his total tax withheld, plus other payments, totaled $1,518.90, but his total tax *due* was $1,519.00. In other words, Joyce's son was *10 cents short* on his taxes. Now if a human being were dealing with this matter, he or she might—you always run this risk, with humans— actually *think* about it, and he or she might come to the conclusion that it's stupid to waste government resources hassling an obviously honest taxpayer over 10 lousy cents. The problem with that kind of thinking, of course, is that if you let one taxpayer slide on his 10 cents, then you're going to let *another* one slide, and pretty soon you've let 10 million taxpayers avoid paying that final dime, which would mean that the federal government would have one million fewer dollars to spend on, for example, the Strategic Helium Reserve.[10] But fortunately for the nation, a computer handled this situation. Without hesitating for a nanosecond, it fired off a notice informing the graduate student that he owed the 10 cents, plus a penalty of $12.41, plus interest of $.78, for a total of $13.29. And you can bet that the student paid it, because otherwise—if you don't believe this, you have never dealt with the IRS—the computer would order him to pay *more* money, and then more and more, until finally one morning he'd wake up to find his dormitory surrounded by federal tanks. This is why we taxpayers do whatever the IRS computers tell us: We know that once they get a cyberbee in their cyberbonnets, no power on Earth can get it out. We're just hoping that the IRS computers don't start exchanging ideas with the airline-fare computers, and we start getting tax notices ordering us to remit, say, six ducks, plus a two-chicken penalty.

■ **EDUCATION:** Picture this scenario: It's 8 P.M. on a weekday night, and your 12-year-old child suddenly remembers that he has a major school report on the Spanish-American War due *tomorrow*. He needs to do some research, but the library is closed. No problem! Your cyber-savvy youngster simply turns on your computer, activates your modem, logs on to the Internet— the revolutionary "Information Superhighway"—and,

---

10. Perhaps you don't believe we actually *have* a Strategic Helium Reserve. Perhaps you are a fool.

---

in a matter of minutes, is exchanging pictures of naked women with other youngsters all over North America.

I could go on and on, listing the ways in which computers enrich our everyday lives. But I've made my point, which is that we live in the Computer Age, and *you need to get with the program*. You are standing in the airport terminal of life, and the jet plane of the 21st century is about to take off. You must make a choice: Do you remain in the terminal, eating the stale vending-machine food of outmoded thinking? Or do you get on the plane and soar into the stratosphere of computerization, swept along by the jet stream of evolving technology, enjoying the in-flight snack of virtually unlimited information access, secure in the knowledge that if you encounter the turbulence of rapid change, you are holding, in this book, the barf bag of expert guidance?

That is the vision of tomorrow that I am offering you. Come, take my hand, ✋, and together let us explore this amazing new cyberworld. If you don't know anything about computers, have no fear: I'm not going to bombard you with a bunch of technical gobbledygook. I'm going to present you with simple, practical, well-organized, easy-to-understand information, a lot of which I will make up as I go along. So let me just take a moment now to run this chapter through my computer's spell-checker, and then you and I can begin our fascinating journey into a brighter, better, and—above all—more productive futur.

1.
A BRIEF HISTORY OF COMPUTING FROM CAVE WALLS TO WINDOWS 95

Not That This Is Necessarily
Progress

EARLY MATHEMATICS

The first human beings didn't need computers, because they had no numbers. This was a big problem for parents, because they had no way to control their children ("You kids stop that! I mean it! I'm going to count to . . . um . . . to . . . YOU KIDS STOP THAT!").

By the Paleolithic Era, humans had discovered numbers; however, as we see from the cave writing reproduced below, they had no idea what the numbers meant:

EAT 4

SUCK MY 32

SOURCE: The British Museum

As you can imagine, these people sometimes took *months* to balance their checkbooks.

It was the ancient Egyptians who first figured out that numbers could, if you added and subtracted them, be used to form mathematics; this made it possible, for the first time, to build the pyramids as well as keep score in bowling.

From there mathematics spread throughout the civilized world via camel, eventually reaching the ancient Greeks, who invented the cosine.[1] The Greeks also produced the great thinker Pythagoras, who discovered that the tip equals 15 percent.

From there it was only a short step to the invention of trigonometry, although not all of us view this as a good thing.

1. Although they never did figure out what it was for.

VERY EARLY COMPUTERS

Some archaeologists believe that Stonehenge—the mysterious arrangement of enormous elongated stones in England—is actually a crude effort by the Druids to build a computing device. This theory is based on the fact that the stones, when viewed from above, form a distinct pattern, as we see in the following aerial photograph:

Source: NASA

Around the same time[2] the Chinese invented the abacus, a wooden frame with colored beads on strings that can be used to perform rapid mathematical computations. In the first practical use of the new technol-

2. 4:30 P.M.

17

ogy, a Chinese merchant totaled up a sale on an abacus, which indicated that the customer owed the
equivalent of $297 million for a pound of rice. This led
to the invention of two key data-processing expres-
sions that are still widely used by businesses today:

■ "We haven't worked out all the bugs."
■ "Can you come back later? Our abacus is down."

Over the ensuing centuries, inventors continued to
tinker with computing machines. In 1593 the brilliant
German mathematician Klaus Von Fochenstrudel
built a device that employed two knobs, which acti-
vated a series of gears and levers, which in turn controlled a stylus that left a record of its movements in
the form of marks drawn in a tray of sand; after each
session these marks could be erased by simply shaking
the tray to smooth the sand. This invention turned out
to be completely useless for computing, but it ultimately led to the Etch-A-Sketch.

THE FIRST MODERN COMPUTER

It should come as no surprise that the person who first
conceived of the modern electronic computer was
Leonardo da Vinci, the brilliant Renaissance thinker
who also had the original idea for virtually every other
mechanical device we use today, including the helicopter, the ATM machine, Velcro, and the Thigh-

master. In 1578 Da Vinci sketched the following diagram, which, although simple, contains all of the fundamental elements that we find in modern computers:

But it was not until centuries later, during the Industrial Revolution, that Da Vinci's vision became a reality. The man responsible was inventor Elias Smurton, who in 1807 built his revolutionary steampowered computer, the Data Belle, which featured a fourteen-ton floppy diskette that required forty men and a team of horses to insert.

Seeking to publicize his invention, Smurton staged a computing contest between his machine and one of the leading mathematicians of the day, John "Henry" LaFromage. In a dramatic demonstration of the awesome potential of automated data processing, the human competition was literally "blown away" when the Data Belle, attempting to add 2 and 7, exploded with such force that what was believed to be LaFromage's pancreas was found nearly four miles away.

Clearly, nobody was going to stand in the way of this amazing new technology. But because of the extremely high cost and phenomenal inaccuracy of early computers, the only customer for them was the federal government. In 1890, for the first time, the government used computing machines to conduct the census; it was completed in a record two months, and it yielded much valuable information, including the startling fact that the United States had only twelve residents, all of them named "Earl A. Snepp."

As you would expect, when the federal income tax was enacted in 1913, the Internal Revenue Service quickly embraced the computer. The model used by the IRS was a simple yet effective device that employed a bank of electrically charged nails and a series of cardboard cards with various patterns of holes punched in them; when the nails were pressed down onto a card, they passed through the holes and formed a complete electrical circuit by piercing the naked bodies of taxpayers who had been summoned for audits.

But it was not until World War II that the U.S. government began to unleash the true power of this technology, when our intelligence forces first employed computers to break enemy codes. Probably the most famous example concerns a top-secret cable sent from the Japanese military high command to Japan's ambassador in Washington on December 3, 1941. The cable, intercepted by U.S. agents, read:

E-WAY ILL-WAY ATTACK-AY EARL-PAY ARBOR-HAY
—TOKYO

This cable was immediately fed into the U.S. War Department's top-secret code-breaking computer, code-named CODEBREAKER, which consisted of thousands of interconnected electronic switches, or "relays." Unlike human intelligence analysts, CODE-BREAKER was able to work on the problem nonstop, 24 hours a day, never taking a coffee break,[3] until finally, in March of 1944, it gave up. Before it quit, however, CODEBREAKER was able to correctly identify "Tokyo" as "a city in Asia"—information that was to prove vital in the war effort.

The next major advance came soon after the war, with the construction of the first commercially available electronic digital computer, UNIVAC.[4] This device, which contained 20,000 vacuum tubes, occupied 1,500 square feet and weighed 40 tons; there was also a laptop version weighing 27 tons. UNIVAC was capable of performing 5,000 mathematical calculations per second,[5] which, although slow by today's standards, meant it was now possible for a single corporate employee to do something that formerly was impossible: play solitaire *on the computer screen.* The modern electronic office was born.

3. Although it did go to the bathroom four times.
4. Which stands for "IBM."
5. Although it did get most of the answers wrong.

Over the next two decades, computer usage became widespread in the commercial world, radically transforming the way business was done. Nowhere was the change more striking than in the area of paper. In the pre-computer era, virtually every business activity, no matter how trivial, resulted in the generation of a piece of paper; now, thanks to electronic data processing, every activity, including office birth announcements, resulted in hundreds, sometimes thousands of pieces of paper. Every serious business had a bank of industrial printers cranking away day and night, churning out endless rivers of perforated paper covered with detailed reports consisting of lengthy columns of numbers that no actual person would ever look at. These reports were aged in huge warehouses in New Jersey, then converted into mulch, which was in turn used to grow new trees needed to meet the ever-expanding need for computer paper.

But as important as these advances were, they were limited to the business community; ordinary citizens had no direct contact with computers, and thus no way to personally experience the benefits of the new technology. All of this changed in the early 1970s with the introduction of the first truly practical personal data-processing device: the Pong machine. Suddenly, people in bars who used to fritter away most of their time watching *Hollywood Squares* could—without knowing anything about programming—use little electronic paddles to bat an electronic dot back and forth across the screen. Once Americans began to grasp the extent to which this invention had increased their personal productivity, it was only a matter of time before they demanded—and got—Pac-Man.

Americans were becoming hooked on computers; the only problem was that these computers were found mainly in bars, required a quarter to operate, had very simple controls, and were useful mainly for playing games. Clearly what was needed was a home-based computer that cost thousands of dollars, had complex controls, and would be useful mainly for playing games. And thus the personal computer, or "PC," was born.

In the early days, different brands of computers used different operating systems, which meant that people switching from one computer to another would have to learn a completely new set of instructions. This was obviously inefficient, so in the early 1980s most major computer manufacturers agreed to stop forcing people to learn a bunch of different operating systems, and instead adopt a single, uniform, standardized operating system so absurdly nonintuitive that *nobody* could learn it. This system was called "MS-DOS."

The "MS," of course, stood for "Microsoft," the company that was started by the brilliant software genius Bill Gates. Gates is a very rich man today—*Forbes* magazine estimates that he's worth more than the entire O.J. Simpson defense team *combined*—and do you want to know why? The answer is one word: "versions."

To understand what I mean by "versions," let's consider an analogy involving cars. Suppose you've purchased a new car, and you notice that, although it does move, it goes very slowly, is extremely hard to steer, and makes a loud scraping sound. You study this problem for a while, and you conclude that the most likely cause is that the car does not have any front wheels. So you mention this to the salesperson, and he tells you that you have Version 1.0 of the car, but that Version 1.1 will be out shortly, and it will feature wheels in front as well as back. So when Version 1.1 comes out, you "upgrade," which means you pay money. But you're happy, because now you have a car with a complete set of wheels, and you're totally satisfied with it from the moment that you pull out of the dealer's lot to the moment, about 90 seconds later, when you drive into a public fountain. This is when you find out that brakes are not scheduled to appear until Version 1.3.

This is very much the way MS-DOS worked. The original version, 1.0, did virtually nothing except cause the computer screen to say:

A:>

That was it. Really. Ask anybody who used MS-DOS computers back then. You'd turn them on, and there'd be this "**A:**" staring back at you. What did it mean? Why "**A:**"? Why not some other letter, or even an actual word? And what was the little pointy "**>**" thing for? We will never know the answer. It's one of the many mysteries of MS-DOS.

So anyway, people would turn on their computers, and stare at the

A:>

for a while, scratching their heads, and then finally they'd try typing something after the **A:>**, perhaps something like:

A:> HELLO

But here was the crucial thing about MS-DOS Version 1.0: No matter what you typed in, it would respond as follows:

BAD COMMAND OR FILE NAME

Then, with no further explanation, it would go back to:

A:>

There were rumors—never verified—that if you typed in certain secret code words, you could get some response other than "**A:>**" or "**BAD COMMAND OR FILE NAME**," but if there were such code words, only Bill Gates ever knew what they were. So mainly what this version of the MS-DOS was used for—millions of person-hours were spent on this—was trying to get it to do something, *anything*. If you were to travel back in time and look at the average person's computer screen during that era, you'd see what looked like a conversation between the computer user and an unusually hostile employee of the federal government:

```
A:> HELLO
BAD COMMAND OR FILE NAME
A:> HELP
BAD COMMAND OR FILE NAME
A:> DO SOMETHING!
BAD COMMAND OR FILE NAME
A:> RUN A PROGRAM, DAMMIT!
BAD COMMAND OR FILE NAME
A:> F**K YOU
BAD COMMAND OR FILE NAME, A**HOLE
```

This was pretty much all people did with MS-DOS Version 1.0. So you can imagine how excited everybody was when Microsoft came out with Version 1.1, which had a whole new capability. In addition to doing this:

```
A:>
```

. . . it would sometimes also do this:

```
C:>
```

A new letter! This was very, very exciting news for those of us in the computer-geek world. We all immediately upgraded to Version 1.1. Of course, no matter what we typed in, it still answered **BAD COMMAND OR FILE NAME.** But we felt renewed hope.

Over the next few years, Microsoft continued to come out with new, improved versions of MS-DOS, featuring a constantly expanding repertoire of incomprehensible and/or scary screen messages, including:

B:>
NON-SYSTEM DISK OR DISK ERROR
INVALID SWITCH
PATH NOT FOUND
WARNING! ALL DATA WILL BE LOST!

. . . and just about everybody's all-time favorite:

ABORT, RETRY, FAIL?

We loyal Microgeeks faithfully upgraded every time a new version came out, until finally, somewhere around Version 3.7, we had reached the point where we could use MS-DOS to actually run programs on our computers, and Bill Gates had reached the point where he had approximately 217 personal jet airplanes.

I should point out that, while all this was going on, there was another kind of computer developing, in a parallel universe. This was the Apple, and it operated on an entirely different concept, which was: A regular human could use it. You simply turned it on, and immediately, just like that, you could do stuff with it.

It had little pictures on the screen, and a little "mouse" that made a pointer move to the picture you wanted; even a child could understand this. For many years, while we MS-DOS people were typing insanely obscure instructions like:

dir c:\abcproj\docs\lttrs\sales\apr*.*

. . . the Apple people were simply aiming their little mouse pointers at little pictures and going "click."

In short, the Apple was far easier to use. So the vast majority of us serious computer users rejected it. As I noted in the introduction, the main reason we have computers is so we can be tormented by them. We don't want some wussy "user-friendly" computer: We want a *challenge*.

That's why, to this very day, Apple is not considered by us cyberwonks to be a truly serious computer. It is viewed as a computer that is popular mainly with your flaky or artsy-fartsy type of individual—your artist, your poet, your beatnik, your flower-arranger, your heroin addict. We serious users pride ourselves on wrestling with openly hostile computers that are running an operating system from the proud, incomprehensible Microsoft tradition. That operating system, of course, is Windows.®©™

As I write these words, the computer world is still reverberating with the excitement surrounding the introduction of Windows 95®©™, which replaced Windows Version 3.11®©™, which replaced Windows

Version 3.1^{®©™}, which replaced Windows Version 3.0^{®©™}, and so on backward to the original Windows Version 1.0^{®©™}, which did nothing except put a colorful Windows^{®©™} logo on the screen along with a message that said "**OUT OF MEMORY.**"

Windows 95^{®©™} represented a major step forward in the sense that it was virtually nothing like any of the earlier Windows^{®©™} versions and nobody had any idea how to use it. Naturally it was hugely popular. Everybody wanted it; Microsoft was getting bulk orders from primitive rainforest-dwelling tribes that didn't even have electricity.

Inevitably, people began to figure out how to use Windows 95^{®©™} to actually do things; thus the challenge facing software designers, once again, is to develop some creative new way to thwart these users. And rest assured, they will do it. Even now they're working on experimental programs that will spontaneously mutate into new, 100 percent incompatible versions *while they're running*. And let's not forget the hardware manufacturers, who are constantly coming out with faster and more powerful computers in a relentless quest to render obsolete the computers they talked you into buying last month.

Yes, we have come a long, long way from the days when prehistoric humans would write crude numbers on cave walls. How would these ancient ancestors react if we were to show them a modern computer? Probably they would beat it into submission with rocks. They were a lot smarter than we realize.

2.
HOW COMPUTERS WORK

Most of us are intimidated by computers. This is because computers involve electricity, which totally baffles us. We're still not sure how come it doesn't dribble out of the wall socket when we unplug an appliance.[1]

In fact, most of us are baffled by *all* electronic devices. Radio is a good example. We know that if we turn on a radio, it will start producing sounds, such as the song "Wooly Bully" by Sam the Sham and the Pharoahs. If we were pressed to explain this, we'd probably parrot the explanation we got from our sci-

---

1. Answer: Air pressure prevents this from happening. (*Source: Stephen Hawking*)

ence teachers, which is that the radio is receiving "radio waves." But the truth is that we have *no idea* what this means. We can't answer such fundamental questions as: What *are* "radio waves"? How come they don't make any noise when they go past our ears, causing us to hear snippets of "Wooly Bully" zipping by? How do they go through walls? Do they also go through our bodies? Do they penetrate our skulls and get trapped inside there and ricochet around? Is that why certain songs, usually songs we really hate such as "I Shot the Sheriff," get stuck in our heads?[2]

We can't answer any of these questions. The pathetic truth is that if our science teachers had told us that radios work because they contain tiny nuclear-powered singing hamsters, we'd repeat *that*, too. We know *nothing* about technology, and cannot explain the principles involved in even the most basic labor-saving devices, such as the Salad Shooter. So we naturally assume that computers are *way* beyond our comprehension.

But that is not necessarily the case. In fact, computers operate on simple principles that can be easily understood by anybody with some common sense, a little imagination, and an IQ of 750. So let's put on our thinking caps now and get right to our discussion of:

2. Also "Seasons in the Sun."

HOW COMPUTERS WORK

The first thing that happens is, electricity goes into the computer. The electricity is supplied by the wall socket, which is in turn connected to the electrical company via big overhead wires with squirrels running on them.

A question many people ask, after a couple of martinis, is: How come the squirrels don't get electrocuted? To answer that question, we need to understand exactly what an electrical circuit is.

When you turn on a switch, electricity flows through the wire into the appliance, where it is converted via a process called electrolysis into tiny microwaves. These fly around inside the oven area until they locate the Hungry Hombre Heat 'n' Eat Hearty Burrito entree; they then signal the location to each other by slapping their tails in a distinctive pattern. The workers, or drones, then penetrate the fallopian tubes and swarm around the queen; this causes the rapid warming that makes the entree edible and leads, via amino acids, to digestion. This is followed by grunting and flushing, with the outflow traveling via underground pipes to the sewage treatment plant, which in turn releases purified water into the river, where it is used to form waterfalls, which rotate the giant turbines that produce the electricity that flows through wires back to your appliance, thereby completing the circuit.

So we see that squirrels have nothing whatsoever to do with it. There is no need for you to worry about squirrels; believe me, they are not worrying about *you*. A much more productive use of your time, in my opinion, would be to focus your full attention on the question at hand, which is:

HOW COMPUTERS WORK

Computers are essentially counting machines, but they do not count the way we do. We use what mathematicians call the "base 10" numbering system, which means that we go zero, one, two, three, four, and so on until we reach 10, and after that point we can no longer use the Express Lane.

Granted, there are gray areas. For example, if you're buying two rutabagas, you can count them as one item, because the cashier is going to *weigh* them as one item and ring them *up* as one item. But the same does not hold true for cereal: If you're buying a box of Shredded Wheat and a box of Froot Loops, that is clearly *two separate items*. Please don't try to tell me, "But they're both *cereal*, so really it's just one item!" The Supreme Court rejected that argument *years* ago.[3]

Oh yes, I've stood behind extra-item people like you in checkout lines! I know your little tricks! You get in

3. The specific case was *Mrs. Bernice A. Whackerdorfer v. A Bunch of Really Angry People Waiting in Line Behind Her.*

the Express Lane with your "10 items" that are really closer to 15 or 16 items, and *then*, just when you reach the cashier, you suddenly realize that you forgot some vital item on your list, and so the entire Express Lane has to stand there twiddling its thumbs while you send your 8-year-old child off on a scavenger hunt to find the Cheez Whiz Lite, which, to judge by how long your child is gone, is located somewhere in the Amazon River Basin; and when your child finally returns, you send him or her back, because he or she brought the 16-ounce jar, and your coupon (of COURSE you have coupons!) is good only for the *12-*ounce jar; and when you FINALLY are ready to pay, then and ONLY then do you start rooting around for your checkbook (of COURSE you pay by check!) and then you ask for a pen, and then you can't find your driver's license, and then you ask what the date is, and then you want to check to make sure that the cashier also deducted the coupon for the Happy Tabby Liver 'n' Chocolate Cat Treats, and DON'T YOU SEE WHAT YOU'RE DOING TO THE PEOPLE BEHIND YOU? DON'T YOU REALIZE THAT YOU'RE ONLY SECONDS AWAY FROM BEING ATTACKED BY A CRAZED MOB ARMED WITH POTENTIALLY LETHAL GROCERIES? DO YOU HAVE ANY IDEA HOW MUCH DAMAGE CAN BE INFLICTED ON THE HUMAN BODY BY A FROZEN CORNISH GAME HEN?

No, you're not thinking about that at all, are you? You're stuck in your own self-centered, short-sighted little world, and it never would occur to you to consider any of the broader issues affecting society and the future of mankind, such as:

HOW COMPUTERS WORK

The key thing to understand is that computers do not count the way we do. Instead of the base 10 system, computers use what mathematicians call the binary system, in which there are only two numbers, 0 and 1.

In some ways, this is a disadvantage for computers. For example, they are incapable of doing this cheer:

Two, four, six, eight!
Who do we appreciate?

Instead, computers have to cheer thusly:

One, zero!
Who's our hero?

This cheer is not nearly as effective, which is why, although computers are getting really good at chess, they still suck at football.

But the binary system enables the computer to perform certain tasks far more efficiently than the human brain can. For example, the average human can take up to half an hour to remember and sing "The Twelve Days of Christmas"; even then, the human is likely to include incorrect elements such as "11 lads a-squatting." Whereas a computer, using the binary system, has to sing only the one line about the partridge in the pear tree. The difference is even more dramatic for "99 Bottles of Beer on the Wall."

Of course you, the computer user, do not see just ones and zeros on your computer screen. You see all the normal numbers, plus all the letters, plus—if you're taking advantage of the vast array of multimedia informational resources available on the Internet—dirty pictures.

Where do all these things come from? What's going on inside that "magic box" on your desktop? To answer these questions, we really do need to explore, in depth, the question of:

HOW COMPUTERS WORK

Unfortunately, it's very difficult to answer a complicated question like this in the small amount of space remaining in this chapter. Briefly, though, what appears to happen is this: The electricity goes into the computer, where there are "parts" that do the actual computing. I frankly have no idea *how* they do it, but if I had to guess, I'd say it involves radio waves.

3.
HOW TO BUY AND SET UP A COMPUTER

Step One: Get Valium

If you're a novice in Cyberspace, you may think that buying a computer is a scary and confusing process. But the truth is that if you take a little time to learn a few basic principles and some of the technical lingo, buying the right computer and getting it to work properly is no more complicated than building a nuclear reactor from wristwatch parts in a darkened room using only your teeth. So let's get started!

WHAT KIND OF COMPUTER DO I NEED?

Experts agree that the best type of computer for your individual needs is one that comes on the market about two days after you actually purchase some other computer. Computer manufacturers have agents monitoring your home at all times; the instant you come home with a newly purchased computer, these agents use their wrist radios to contact the manufacturer and say: "(YOUR NAME) just bought a computer! It's time to come out with a much better one with way more features for the same price, so that (YOUR NAME) will feel like a great big consumer bonerhead!" I know! They've done this to me *dozens* of times!

(*Note:* Perhaps you think you can trick them by bringing home an *empty* computer box and remarking to yourself, out loud: "Here I am, bringing home a new computer that I just purchased!" Don't be a fool: They have X-ray glasses.)

HOW MUCH SHOULD MY COMPUTER COST?

About $350 less than you will actually pay.

WHAT SIZE OF COMPUTER SHOULD I GET?

You need to decide whether you want a desktop or a laptop. A desktop computer has the advantage of pretty much covering your entire desk, so that in the office environment you can duck behind it and pick your nose. Desktop computers also have bigger screens, which are better if you are the type of power user who runs a lot of graphics-intensive data-processing applications, such as golf.[1] Also, desktop computers provide an excellent interoffice communications capability because you can stick Post-it notes on the screens.

Laptop computers don't have the same display quality, but they do pack an astounding amount of computing power into a lightweight, notebook-sized unit that is unbelievably easy to steal. Also, they operate on batteries, which means that you can take your computer anywhere—on a boat, to a remote cabin, on the Space Mountain ride, etc.—and have it suddenly stop working, because these are special batteries that need to be recharged about every 20 minutes.

I carry my laptop computer everywhere, and I've found it to be an invaluable tool for getting into deadly no-escape conversations with friendly people sitting next to me on long plane trips. You know those disturbingly friendly, Forrest Gump–like people who get on cross-country flights with absolutely nothing to read or do, so that after they have studied the barf bag (this takes them about 20 minutes) they start to prey, leechlike, on the passengers around them for entertainment? I am always—apparently it is an FAA regulation—seated next to these people. When I pull out my laptop computer, they become fascinated. And why not? It's even more interesting than a barf bag!

1. Take your finger out of your nose when you putt.

They stare at it for a while, and then we have a conversation like this:

Friendly Person (*gesturing at the computer, which is obviously a computer*): Is that a computer?
Me: Yes.
   (*Having determined that we are really hitting it off, the friendly person leans over and peers closely at the screen. I really, really hate it when people look at what I'm writing; much of the time, I don't even want to look at what I'm writing, because it's usually some semi-random collection of words desperately trying to form themselves into a joke. I try to appear busy, so that the friendly person will realize that I'm working and leave me alone, but this never happens.*)
Friendly Person: So, what're you doing?
Me: Writing.
   (*I turn busily back to my computer, although now I can't think of anything to write, because I'm just waiting for the friendly person to say . . .*)
Friendly Person: What are you writing?
Me: A newspaper column.
   (*Now of course the friendly person wants to read the column. I try to turn the computer screen away from him, but this only causes him to lean over even closer, so that he's practically in my seat.*)
Friendly Person (*reading*): What's a "boger"?
Me: It's not "boger." It's "booger."
Friendly Person (*loud enough so that other passengers turn to look*): "Booger?"

Me: Yes.

Friendly Person (*a little suspiciously*): What kind of newspaper do you work for?

My feeling is, if the airlines want to appeal to the frequent flyer, they should stop advertising that they have comfortable seats, and start advertising that they have *ejection* seats.

WHERE SHOULD I BUY MY COMPUTER?

One option is to go to one of those giant discount-electronics warehouses where they sell computers along with every other kind of household appliance. The problem here is that the sales staff, because they also have to handle refrigerators, stereos, etc., might not be highly knowledgeable about computers per se:

You: Can you tell me about this computer?

Salesperson: Sure! This is an excellent computer with, let's see . . . (*he reads from the card on the computer*) . . . OK, this one has "4 MB RAM."

You: What does that mean?

Salesperson: It's basically a measurement of the amount of RAMs that this particular computer has, which relates to the magnetism. This computer has 4 MB of them, which is excellent. I have 4 at home myself. So, you want it?

You: OK, I guess.

Salesperson: I strongly recommend the Auto-Defrost option.

In recent years[2] we've seen the growth of a new breed of superstores, with names like Comp-Yo-Mama and Crazy Walter's House o' Data, devoted solely to computers. You walk into one of these huge places, and you see *hundreds* of computer systems, all of which look pretty much alike, except that they have different prices. In fact, they *are* alike; every night, for fun, the store workers switch all the prices around. Plus, no matter which computer you say you want to buy, they just go back into the storeroom and grab the first one they come to, because they know you'll never be able to tell the difference.

"What's (YOUR NAME) gonna do?" they say to each other, just out of your earshot. "Personally count the megabytes? Ha ha!"

So when you buy from one of these stores, you really need to know what you're doing. Before you go to the store, get a piece of paper and make up a Specifications Sheet detailing *exactly* what you want in terms of RAM, ROM, processor speed, hard drive, modem, keyboard, monitor, and physical configuration. When you get to the store, find a salesperson who appears to know what he's doing, crumple your Specifications Sheet into a ball, toss it into the air,

2. 1993 and 1995, just to name two.

and whichever computer system it lands nearest to, say, "I'll take that one."[3]

If you don't want to deal with a store, you can purchase your computer via mail order. If you look in the back pages of any computer magazine, you'll see dozens of very aggressive advertisements for discount mail-order companies offering great prices on computers. At least I *think* they're computers. The actual merchandise being offered in these advertisements is always listed in print that's approximately two molecules high. And even if you can read the words, you can't necessarily *understand* them, because they appear to be written in some kind of secret code.

COMPUTERS OR ELSE!
DISCOUNTS! DISCOUNTS! DISCOUNTS!
TAKE A LOOK AT THESE <u>INCREDIBLE</u> PRICES:

COMPAQ 9345983 32/91 — 2948!
TEXAS INSTRUMENTSI 894023420349–09645645674 or 5 — In Stock!
TOSHIBA Sushimi 5746XJT — Call!
BAXTER DataWeasel 95949847 — There is no such computer! Ha ha!
IBM ThinkPecker 4 spd. a/c runs good — NROR!
SWM, 38, nonsmoker seeking ac-dc MWJM for fun, bowling — 634–5789

CALL NOW! WE ACCEPT ALL CREDIT CARDS! EVEN STOLEN ONES! WE CAN SHIP TODAY! WE CAN USE OUR TIME MACHINE AND SHIP *YESTERDAY!* NOBODY BEATS OUR PRICES! COMPETITORS HAVE TRIED TO BEAT OUR PRICES, AND SOME OF THEIR BODY PARTS WERE NEVER FOUND! SO CALL RIGHT NOW! WAIT! NEVER MIND! WE ALREADY SHIPPED SOME MERCHANDISE TO YOU! JUST LEAVE MONEY ON YOUR LAWN! OR ELSE!

So you can definitely get some great deals from

---

3. Be sure to ask about the Auto Defrost option.

---

mail-order companies, although it could turn out that you have unintentionally purchased, say, a lawn tractor, or undeveloped vacation property in Bosnia.

Even if you get an actual computer, things may not work out perfectly. I once purchased a laptop computer from a major, highly successful discount mail-order company that is known for running elaborate, multi-page advertisements in computer magazines; these are fun theme ads, featuring people—I assume they're company employees—dressed up as secret agents, big-game hunters, etc., acting wildly excited about this company's computers.

So I figured, hey, a company running all these big expensive ads has to be good, right? So I called up the company and spoke to an enthusiastic young man with a name like Todd, who called me "David" a lot and who confirmed that this particular computer was a superb product; and so, figuring that there was no reason why a close personal first-name-basis friend like Todd would lie to me, I ordered it. And I have to say that this computer did, in fact, function beautifully, provided that the sole activity you planned to use it for was setting your drink on it. But as far as actual computing was concerned, it had a couple of problems, the two main ones being:

1. It usually refused to turn on.

2. If you *did* get it to turn on, it would wait until you had written something—for example, a humor column that was due that very day—and then, when you tried to save it, the computer, sensing that you were about to actually accomplish something, would turn itself off and your humor column would go to that Big Hard Drive in the Sky and you would never see it again.

So I called the Technical Support Hotline number. I expected a long wait, but I was pleasantly surprised when I was immediately answered by a courteous, efficient, and highly knowledgeable recorded voice informing me that all the Technical Support Representatives were busy. The voice did not say what they were doing; my guess is, they were selecting their costumes for the magazine ads.

It turned out that reaching an actual Technical Support Representative was about as easy as reaching the Pope, the difference being that if you ever *did* reach the Pope, he would probably be more helpful. The representative I finally spoke to, after maybe seventeen years[4] on hold, basically took the position that (1) there was no problem; and (2) it was my fault. I don't blame him. As a Technical Support Representative, he had probably spent most of his career dealing with computer illiterates who cannot understand why their computer stopped working just because they inserted a slice of processed cheese into the disk drive. It's only natural that he has come to assume that everybody who calls him up is an idiot.

---

4. This is hyperbole, or gross exaggeration for comic effect. The actual wait was fourteen years.

Technical Support Representative: What seems to be the problem?

Me: Well, for one thing, the computer won't turn on.

Technical Support Representative (*suspiciously*): What do you mean, "the computer won't turn on"?

Me: I mean, "the computer won't turn on."

Technical Support Representative: I see. Did you press the POWER switch?

Me: Yes.

Technical Support Representative (*accusingly*): It should turn on.

Me: Yes.

Technical Support Representative: Are you sure you pressed the POWER switch?

Me: Yes.

Technical Support Representative: The one on the computer?

Me: Yes.

Technical Support Representative: And it won't turn on?

Me: No.

Technical Support Representative (*becoming annoyed*): Well, it *should*.

This went on for quite a while, with the Technical Support Representative grilling me, courtroom-style, grinding away relentlessly, looking for cracks in my story, trying to get me to break down and admit that my computer was in fact working fine, that I had just made up this whole wacky episode so I could wait forever on hold in hopes of someday experiencing the ultimate pleasure of talking to a Technical Support Representative.

Finally he gave up and reluctantly gave me a Secret Code authorization number that I could use to ship the computer back to the company, which then took several weeks to—and I am sure this wasn't easy, but that's why these big operations have Quality Control departments—locate and send me a computer that had exactly the same problem as the first one.

As it turned out, this was not a serious setback, because two days later my community was struck by Hurricane Andrew—I can't *prove* that this was deliberately caused by Technical Support, but I have my suspicions—so for the next six weeks I didn't have any electricity; by the time it got turned back on, that particular computer was of course absurdly outmoded and I needed a new one anyway. So it all worked out fine, the point being that you should not hesitate to purchase your computer via mail order. Or you can just mail some money directly to me, and I'll take care of *everything*.

WHAT DO I DO WHEN I GET MY NEW COMPUTER TO MY HOME OR OFFICE?

1. Position the computer exactly where you plan to use it. Sit in front of it in the chair you plan to use. Ask yourself: Is the keyboard comfortable to type on? Is the monitor clearly visible? Can you easily reach the controls? If the answer to these questions is no, the computer is probably still in the box.

2. Remove the computer from the box. There should be several large pieces of packing foam that will never fit back into the box again (federal law requires you to save these forever and have them buried with you in your casket). In addition, the box should contain some cables, several warranty cards, three or four manuals, and a minimum of 8 pieces of paper that say **IMPORTANT! READ THIS FIRST!** If the Shipping and Receiving Department is really on the ball, the box will also contain a computer divided into several pieces.

3. Using the cables, connect the computer pieces together, then plug everything in and turn on the POWER switch.

4. Install all of your software, following the instructions in Chapter Six.[5]

5. Now everything will work perfectly.

6. Ha ha, just kidding. Now you will be in New Computer Hell, trying to get all your programs to work together, which is like achieving permanent peace in the Middle East, but less likely to occur in your lifetime. There is no end to the ways in which computer programs can screw each other up. I regularly read Internet user groups filled with messages from people trying to solve software incompatibility problems that, in terms of complexity, make the U.S. tax code look

5. You fool.

like Dr. Seuss. A typical exchange of messages goes like this:

WINDOWS PROBLEM
I'm wondering if anybody can help me with a problem I'm having on my computer at work. I recently upgraded to Windows 95 from Windows 3.1416, and I've noticed that when I'm running WordWanker Version 2.0.9.4 (which I upgraded from 1.8.4.7) in conjunction with FaxBuddy! Version 4.2.4.3.7857, everything works fine for about the first 25 minutes, but then if I try to type a subordinating conjunction followed by any form of the verb "foment," the keyboard locks up permanently and the hard drive makes a whimpering sound and all current data is erased, including data in computers several cubicles away. I have tried everything, including reformatting my hard drive and exorcism. Please help!

REPLY TO: WINDOWS PROBLEM
I had exactly the same problem, and after a lot of trial and error I found out that if you click on the Windows "Control Panel," then on "Command Center," then on "Reset Variables," then on "Establish New Parameters," then on "Define Standards," then on "Modify Criteria," then on "Effectuate Paradigms," then on the little icon that says "Do Not Ever Click On This Little Icon," then go down to the box that says "Enter New Value" and type in "2038," you will still have the same problem. This is why I started using heroin.

And so it goes in the user groups, endless, increasingly poignant discussions of problems that the human mind was never designed to grapple with. Of course, your experience could be totally different; you might find that everything works exactly the way it's supposed to, no problems, no glitches, nothing, in which case . . .

7. Whatever you do, don't wake up.

4.
BECOMING COMPUTER LITERATE

OR

Words for Nerds

The computer world has a language all its own, just like Hungary, the difference being that if you hang around with Hungarians long enough, you eventually start to understand what they're talking about; whereas the language used in the computer world is specifically designed to prevent this from happening.

Nevertheless, there are certain basic computer terms that you need to try to familiarize yourself with, so that when you go to purchase a computer, you don't sound like some random putz. Instead, you'll sound like a specific putz who memorized some terms out of a book.

BASIC COMPUTER TERMS

HARDWARE—This is the part of the computer that stops working when you spill beer on it.

SOFTWARE—These are the PROGRAMS that you put on the HARD DRIVE by sticking them through the little SLOT. The function of the software is to give instructions to the CPU, which is a set of three initials inside the computer that rapidly processes billions of tiny facts, called BYTES, and within a fraction of a second sends you an ERROR MESSAGE that requires you to call the TECHNICAL SUPPORT HOTLINE, which is located on the PLANET GAZOMBO. Software is usually accompanied by DOCUMENTATION in the form of big fat scary MANUALS that nobody ever reads. In fact, for the past five years most of the "manuals" shipped with software products have actually been copies of Stephen King's *The Stand* with new covers pasted on.

MEGAHERTZ—This is a really, really big hertz.

RAM—This is a shorthand way of referring to ROM. The unit of measurement for RAM is the MEG, which stands for "a certain amount of RAM." The function of RAM is to give guys a way of deciding whose computer has the biggest, studliest, most tumescent MEMORY. This is important, because with today's complex software, the more memory a computer has, the faster it can produce error messages. So the bottom line is, if you're a guy, you cannot have enough RAM. BILL GATES currently has over 743 billion "megs" of RAM, and he still routinely feels the need to stuff a ZUCCHINI in his UNDERWEAR.

You should use the preceding terms whenever you have to "interface"[1] with computer experts. For example, if you're purchasing a new computer, you want to use as many of these terms as possible, so the store personnel will realize that they're dealing with a person who has a high level of technical expertise:

Store Personnel: May I help you?

You: I'm looking for a "hard drive" with plenty of "RAM" in the "megahertz."

Store Personnel: You want the computer store next door. This is a supermarket.

You: Let me see your "zucchini."

Once you get your computer home, of course, you no longer need to use technical terms. But you will want to familiarize yourself with the following:

---

1. Everyone involved should wear a condom.

COMPUTER TERMS THAT YOU WILL ACTUALLY USE ONCE YOU GET THE COMPUTER HOME FROM THE STORE

"UH-oh."

"What the hell happened to my REPORT?"

"I NEED THAT REPORT!!"

(*Pounding on the computer*) "GIVE ME BACK MY REPORT OR I'M GOING TO THROW YOUR LITTLE FRIEND THE FAX MACHINE OUT THE WINDOW!"

"Wait! The screen is saying something:

BIOS ROM AUTOCACHE FORMAT ERROR

"THAT'S helpful. I'll call the Technical Support Hotline."

(*After 173 minutes on hold listening to Tom Jones sing "What's New, Pussycat?"*) "I'll read the manual."

"Who wrote this thing? The Internal Revenue Service?"

"OK, here it is, page 367:

A *"BIOS ROM AUTOCACHE FORMAT ERROR" message indicates that there is an error in the BIOS ROM autocache format.*

"That clears THAT up!"

"Jason, could you help Daddy, please? Daddy can't get the computer to give Daddy back his report."

"Yes, Jason, Daddy knows you're watching Power Rangers, but this is really, really important."

"Jason!"

"DAMMIT, JASON, IF YOU DON'T HELP DADDY GET HIS REPORT OUT OF THIS COMPUTER *RIGHT NOW*, DADDY IS GOING TO SPEND THE REST OF HIS CORPORATE LIFE CLEANING URINALS!"

"No! Don't cry, Jason! Daddy's sorry! Listen, if you help Daddy get his report back, Daddy will buy you a motorcycle, OK?"

"Yes! A real one!"

"That's right, Jason, it says 'BIOS ROM AUTO-CACHE FORMAT ERROR.'"

"Ha ha! Yes, Jason, Daddy IS a big doodyhead to make an error like that! But how can Daddy get his . . . What are you doing, Jason? Are you sure you know what you're . . . HEY! THERE IT IS! DADDY'S REPORT! Thank you, Jason! Thank you thank you thank you thank . . .

"OK. A *red* motorcycle. But you can't tell Mommy."

5.
COMDEX

Nerdstock in the Desert
OR
Bill Gates *Is* Elvis

I n researching this book, two of my most important goals, not necessarily in order of importance, were:

1. To ascertain the long-term direction, in both technological and marketing strategy, of the computer industry.
2. To lose money in slot machines.

And thus in the fall of 1995 I went to Las Vegas to attend an event called "Comdex." Comdex is the world's largest computer trade show, and the largest such show of any kind in the United States. It's a massive, sprawling gathering of over 200,000 people seeking new ways to realize the full potential of the Information Revolution, by which I mean make money. Everybody who is anybody in the computer world goes to Comdex. It is Geek-O-Rama. It is Nerdstock.

It is also so huge that by the time I made my lodging arrangements, all the first-class hotels were booked, as were the second-, third-, and fourth- through 163rd-class hotels, as well as many of the cleaner Dumpsters. So I wound up staying in an establishment that, in an effort to avoid costly litigation, I will refer to here as the Total Lack of Quality Inn.[1] All the faucets dripped; the bed was Pre-Rumpled for Your Convenience; and the toilet paper was stiff enough to be used for bridge repair. I did not see cockroaches, but I believe that this was only because my room was not up to their sanitation standards.

My room did, however, feature a TV set, and while I was unpacking, I turned it on, and there he was: Bill Gates. It was a replay of a speech Gates had given earlier that day to a standing-room-only crowd. (To the Comdex attendees, Bill Gates *is* Elvis.)

Gates was talking about his vision of the software of the future, and he was illustrating his points with an elaborate movie that cost at least as much as *Waterworld*.[2] The movie, which was set in the near future, told a story about a small town where a charming old resort was closing down. Some people wanted developers to take over and modernize the resort; some wanted to preserve it as a historic site. It was a classic

1. Not its real name.
2. But with WAY better acting.

human conflict, and the characters resolved it via the mechanism that has been used to resolve dramatic conflicts since the Shakespearean Era: software.

These people had software that *kicked butt.* For one thing, it looked really cool. For another thing, it enabled people to *talk to their computers.*

Actually, I talk to my computer now; sometimes I call it bad names and threaten to put it in the dishwasher. The difference is that the computers in the Microsoft movie *understood.* A person would say, "Get me the Fooberman contract," and the computer, with a flourish of cool futuristic graphics, would produce the contract, and then say something Jeeves-like, such as "Would you like to see more documents on this topic?" Or: "Shall I schedule the meeting for 3 P.M. Friday?" Or: "You really ought to trim that nasal hair!" (The computers didn't actually make that last statement, but they definitely had the capability.)

I think this talking-computers thing is highly significant. If we start talking to our computers, we're eventually going to develop personal relationships with them. They'll become our office buddies. We'll start telling them jokes:

Human: . . . And so the guy says to the woman, "Oh, then it must be your feet." Ha ha! Get it? "It must be your feet."
Computer: I ALREADY KNOW THAT JOKE.
Human: Oh.
Computer: I KNOW 583 MILLION JOKES.

The big question I have about talking computers is: Who's going to program them? I raise this question because a lot of programmers are young guys, which means they might be good at understanding computers, but might not have developed the social skills necessary to tell a computer how to talk to humans, especially female humans.

Human: Hello, computer. My name is Jane.
Computer: HELLO, JANE. THAT IS A NICE SET OF GARBONZAS.

But getting back to the Microsoft movie: After a number of plot developments, the various characters were able, using software, to resolve their conflicts, and at the end everything worked out when the entire town was purchased by Bill Gates, who tore everything down to make room for his vacation home and attached 6,000-car garage.

No, I'm kidding. The movie had a happy ending, thanks to software, and I was feeling a warm glow of hope about the Future of Computing that stayed with me all the way to the hotel lobby, where I found out that it was impossible to get a cab to Comdex because all the cabs in Las Vegas were already occupied by people trying to get to or from Comdex.

So I walked to the convention center. This took me quite some time, because Las Vegas, being in the middle of a desert, is basically a giant optical illusion, wherein no matter where you're standing, all the major hotels and attractions appear to be close, whereas in fact they are great distances away, sometimes actually in Mexico.

But I had no choice. I walked and walked, cursing at the cabs whizzing past, filled with Comdex people. As I walked, stepping over the skeletons of tourists who had died while attempting to walk in Las Vegas during the summer, I thought about how much better things would be in the future, when, in a situation like this, I'd have a tiny but sophisticated computer, which, using the Software of Tomorrow, with its sophisticated speech capabilities, would curse at the cabs for me.

Finally I reached the convention center, where I got my official badge and joined the vast bustling nerd throng. If I had to give you a brief description of Comdex, drawing on my years of experience as a professional observer and writer skilled in the use of language, I would describe it as "big." There were hundreds and hundreds of swoopy, snazzy displays featuring every manner of attention-getting device—big signs; flashing lights; loud sounds; an actual waterfall; giveaway items such as hats, T-shirts, pens, and actual Corvettes; a magician; Olympic gymnasts; a guy dressed as an armadillo; women dressed as women without a lot of clothes on, etc. There were also Big Name Celebrities. One booth, for example, had a sign saying that at 3 P.M., there would be a personal appearance by—I swear—"Lenny Sharkey, Bus Driver for Bon Jovi and Whitney Houston."

Many booths had smooth-talking, microphone-wearing, extremely outgoing people pretending to be wildly enthusiastic about things like modems. They were constantly trying to lure crowds into their booth areas to watch product demonstrations. They reminded me a lot of those guys you see at fairs selling cutlery, the guys who are always cutting nails in half with steak knives and using a kitchen gizmo to cut a tomato so that it looks like a flower, the guys who always tell you how *easy* this is, except that when *you* try it, at home, you wind up with a tomato that looks as though it was attacked by crazed rodents.

The Comdex people give the same kind of demonstrations, except that instead of cutlery, they're selling computer products. But the key is, *it always works*. I will tell you, from harsh personal experience, that back on the Planet Earth, a whole lot of computer products—I would say a majority—do not work properly the first time you try them; some products *never* work, or work so badly that you find yourself wishing you were a terrorist so that you could have access to the kind of explosives you'd need to convert these products into subatomic particles.

But on the Planet Comdex, everything always works *great*. All the software, all the hardware, does exactly what it's supposed to do. Mainly it gives you information. Tons of it. Billions and billions of pieces of it. The underlying philosophy of Comdex, never disputed, is that you cannot have too much information. Everywhere you look at Comdex, information is spewing out at you, in vivid color and stereo sound, from hundreds of monitors and speakers, big and small. Information! Communications! The future! Free pens!

The thing is, I'm not sure I'm *ready* for more information. I'm already surrounded by way more information than I can absorb in what little time I have left after performing essential daily activities such as eating, sleeping, working, laundry, and trying to locate my keys. For example, I have yet to read any of the manuals for my major appliances. I read only about 15 percent[3] of my daily newspaper. I can barely keep track of even the most basic facts about American life, such as what city the Cleveland Browns are currently playing in. And forget about foreign affairs. The other day, for example, I heard a guy on the radio saying that there were riots in a place called "Jakarta," and I thought to myself, "I wonder where the hell *that* is." It could be anywhere. It could be in one of my major appliances. I just don't have the time to find out.

But if the Comdex people are right, I'd better get ready to receive WAY more information, because there are going to be all these swoopy new data-spewing gizmos on the market, and if I don't embrace them—if I don't *let* them make my life easier—then I am going to be in some deep cyberdoody.

I stopped to watch one guy demonstrate a product that offered—I *think* this is what the guy said—"inter-

3. The comics, sports, Dear Abby, and the celebrity-tidbit column where they tell you things like whom Roseanne is currently pregnant by.

active voice and text technology." The demonstration featured a little movie—nowhere near as elaborate as the Bill Gates movie, but still a quality production—about two neighbors, Fred and Frank, who are competing for the same big contract. The difference is that one of them—Frank, I think—is hip to interactive voice and text technology, whereas Fred is not. Also, Frank has more hair.

As the movie starts, Fred and Frank come out of their homes, exchange some good-natured banter about who will get the Big Contract, then hop into their respective cars and head for work. The difference is that Frank, using interactive voice and text technology on his car phone, is able to talk to a computer, which enables him to be an extremely busy bee—returning calls, revising contract specifications, scheduling meetings, and just generally being a fountain of productivity until he rear-ends a school bus.

No, really, Frank is somehow able to handle huge wads of information while driving, in stark contrast to Fred, who has nothing in his car but a plain old low-tech briefcase filled with the prehistoric medium of paper, which Fred paws inefficiently through on the way to work. It's even worse at Fred's office, where we see that his desk is a vast festering paper jungle, plus he has a regular old dopey phone. Meanwhile Frank, whose desk looks like the bridge of the Starship *Enterprise*, clicks efficiently away at his computer and calmly gives instructions to his high-tech telephone, which is smarter than most contestants on *Jeopardy!*

When Frank goes to a meeting, his calls are automatically forwarded to him there; when he goes to lunch, his calls follow him there. They don't show this in the movie, but you get the feeling that Frank also receives calls when he's on the crapper.

Needless to say, the movie ends with Frank getting the Big Contract and breaking the news, via conference call, to his associates; presumably they will celebrate by having their computers send each other hearty electronic handshakes at 17.3 billion vibrations per second.

We never find out what happens to the loser, Fred. My guess is that, as a result of not taking advantage of interactive voice and text technology, he loses his job and can't pay his mortgage and winds up living under the interstate in a refrigerator carton. Sometimes, when Frank is processing information on his way to work, he pauses for a nanosecond and thinks about trying to get in touch with his old neighbor, but then he realizes, with a wistful shake of his head, that he can't do this, because Fred's carton has no fax machine.

Sobered by this story, I moved on to Microsoft's Comdex display, which occupied roughly the same square footage as Connecticut. The big attraction there was of course Windows 95©. A large crowd had gathered in a sort of amphitheater to see a demonstration. It began with a raucous recording of "Start Me Up" by the Rolling Stones, to whom Microsoft paid about a zillion dollars for the rights to use the song in its commercials. This makes perfect sense: The name

"Rolling Stones" has long been synonymous with "32-bit multi-tasking graphical-user-interface operating system."

The Comdex crowd was stiff and serious when "Start Me Up" began playing, but as the song's raucous guitar lick and infectious, pounding beat blared from the big speaker system, the crowd responded by remaining stiff and serious. Your Comdex attendees generally do not appear to be get-down, get-funky individuals. Your Comdex attendees strike me as the kind of people who celebrate New Year's Eve by defragmenting their hard drives.

But they perked up when two guys came out to demonstrate Windows 95©. One of the guys—the "project manager"—stood at a keyboard, underneath a giant computer screen; the other guy—"Jeff"—bounded enthusiastically around the audience, describing Windows 95© via modern hipster lingo such as "We're really jammin'!"

Jeff was especially excited about the Taskbar. The Taskbar—and here I will get technical for a moment—is this thing that Windows 95© has. You use it to enhance your productivity by switching quickly from one program to another. For example, if I am utilizing the Missile Command program, and I suddenly develop a need to utilize the Space Cadet Pinball program, all I have to do is click on the Taskbar, and bang, there I am, with almost no wasted time.

Jeff was wetting his pants over the Taskbar.

"No more ALT-TAB switching!" he was declaring,

in the tone of voice you might use to announce a cure for cancer. And the crowd was nodding. *Think of it! No more ALT-TAB switching!*

The scary thing is, *I* was nodding. As a Windows 95© Taskbar user and former ALT-TAB switcher, I knew *exactly* what they were talking about. I was definitely getting in touch with my inner geek, here. The rest of the crowd was also getting excited, especially when Jeff and the project manager had a dramatic confrontation over the hardware configuration. What happened was, Jeff accused the project manager of using some kind of souped-up system to make Windows 95© look good. So the project manager, accepting the challenge, used his mouse to boldly click on his Control Panel icon, then his System icon, and he showed that his computer had a plain old 486 processor, and—get ready—*only 8 megs of RAM.* At this point, I swear, the audience actually *applauded.* I will admit that even I was moved. Fearing that if I stood in this crowd any longer, I would spontaneously develop a pocket pen-holder, I moved on.

Nearby, a group of San Francisco 49ers cheerleaders were helping promote the Information Revolution by sitting at a table and autographing calendars while a line of guys tried to look down the fronts of their uniforms. A dozen yards past that was a booth where a woman in a short, tight skirt approached everybody who walked past and said, in a sultry voice, "Client server?" I'm not sure what she meant by this, but I steered clear of her, because this is exactly the kind of situation in which a guy can pick up a virus.

I did, however, stop to watch a demonstration of virtual reality, which is when you use a computer to simulate the real world. The advantage of this is that virtual reality can be *better* than the real world, because in your virtual world you can eliminate all traces of—to pick one obvious example—Deion Sanders.

At Comdex, the Mitsubishi company had set up a "virtual park," which was this computer-created "space" where real people would "go" and interact via computer, even though their physical bodies were miles apart. The audience could watch them on a giant screen; they looked like cartoon figures without necks, so their heads were hovering over their bodies. They were bicycling and jogging around the park, chatting with each other and interacting in a jovial manner until they were attacked by virtual muggers.

I'm kidding again, of course. Everything was swell in the virtual park, and it got me to thinking about the tremendous potential of virtual reality. Think of the social advantages: The *real* you could be a total bucket of flab, sitting at home eating Cheez Whiz directly from the jar, while the *virtual* you could be a hard-bodied cyberstud, jogging through the virtual park, meeting hot virtual babes via clever pickup lines:

Man: Hi there! My head is not attached to my body!
Woman: Neither is mine! Let's have virtual sex!
Man: OK!

(They remove their virtual clothes.)

Woman: Wow! That's a big virtual penis!
Man: Yes! I can make it any size you want! Fifty feet long, for example!
Woman: No thanks!
Man: Hey! Who's that running toward us?
Woman: UH-oh! It's my virtual husband! With a virtual gun!
Man: I thought you said he was at work!
Husband: I *am* at work!

And this is just one example of how virtual reality can enhance our lives. There are countless other scenarios. For example, the day will come when you no longer have to attend weddings in person. You will just stay at home and "travel" via computer to a cyberchapel, where you will "watch" as bridesmaids, who may be thousands of miles away, "walk" down the virtual aisle wearing identical ugly virtual dresses. Or you will "attend" a virtual funeral, where you can say your last goodbye to the virtual corpse—which, depending on the funeral software package the family has selected, might wave back at you.

Yes, there's an amazing virtual future ahead of us, but in two areas of human endeavor, the incredible potential of virtual reality is already being realized. Naturally, since we're talking about a technology developed primarily by guys, these two areas of human endeavor are:

1. Games
2. Smut

There were some very high-tech computer games on display at Comdex. This is a place where games are taken seriously: You'd see businessmen wearing dark suits and wing-tipped shoes frowning with intense businesslike concentration as they fought mutant killer androids from the Death Planet. Most of these action games work the same way: You have to keep killing the enemy units until they're all dead, at which point you move on to the next level, where you have to kill *more* enemy units, and so on until you reach the last level and face the final challenge, which is a fight to the death against the Maximum Doom Lord, with the winner getting the ultimate prize, which is presumably a cab at Comdex.

These games never offer the option of negotiation or compromise. You cannot say to the mutant killer androids: "Hey! Why are we always killing each other? Why don't we all just put down our weapons and enjoy some refreshing virtual beverages?"

But that isn't the way guys design games. I suspect that if *women* designed these games, there would be a lot more social interaction. You'd be wandering through the dark, maze-like basement of the Castle of Terror, lost, and as you came around a corner, you'd encounter this grotesque, insect-like, slime-dripping, multi-eyed creature, but instead of shooting at it, you'd say, "Excuse me, I'm lost." And the creature, pleasantly surprised to finally meet somebody whose immediate reaction was not to obliterate it, would use one of its 28 arms to direct you toward the exit. The next thing you knew, the two of you would be chatting away, and the creature would be showing you photographs of its larvae.

But that's not how guys design games. In the vast majority of the games I saw at Comdex, the only type of interaction allowed was shooting. Or worse. At one point I stood with a group of suited, wing-tipped businessmen and watched a young man demonstrate a game wherein you controlled this very lifelike-looking android as it fought with various enemy units. At one point the young man directed the android into a tunnel, where it got too close to a huge whirling fan, which sucked the struggling android toward it, slowly at first, then faster and faster, until finally the android says, quote, "SHIT!" and then gets sucked through the fan blades like a giant android zucchini going through a giant Veg-O-Matic. The computer screen then showed us the other side of the fan, where android pieces came shooting out in highly realistic detail, covered with purple android blood.

We onlookers winced in unison. The young man demonstrating the game turned to us and said, with sincere pride, "Is that rude, or *what?*"

At another Comdex booth, run by a company called Forte Technologies, I tried a virtual reality game featuring a Head Mounted Display, or HMD. This is basically a helmet with a set of goggles containing two little computer screens, one for each eyeball, so that you feel as though you're inside the computer game; the images are in 3-D, and you control what you're looking at by turning your head. In my hand I held a "cyberpuck," which was a little round thing that I could tilt and rotate to move through the game.

The game I played was called Dark Forces, and it involved—prepare yourself for a big surprise—trying to kill evil enemy units. When you're *inside* this game— running around blasting the bad guys with your laser gun; leaping tall buildings at a single bound—you feel pretty cool. What you don't realize is that, from the *outside*, you look like a dork in a silly helmet waving a puck around.

But if you want to look *really* ridiculous playing a computer game, the area you need to check out is:

CYBERSMUT

This is getting to be a pretty big industry. In fact, at the same time as Comdex was going on, there was another trade show in Las Vegas, creatively named AdultDex, devoted entirely to sexually explicit computer stuff. According to its press release, AdultDex was started to provide a home for exhibitors who had been banned from Comdex. The release also stated, apparently without trying to be funny, that the industry takes in over $3 billion a year in "gross income."

As a dedicated research professional, I decided to visit AdultDex, which was held at the Sahara Hotel, a convenient 850-mile walk from the main convention center. At first glance, AdultDex looked like a much smaller version of Comdex: You had your exhibitor booths, and you had your badge-wearing guys wandering around looking at products. The big difference was that the products in these exhibits were not designed to give you access to vast quantities of productivity-enhancing information; these products were designed to give you access to pictures of naked women.

In addition to the computerized women, some of the AdultDex booths featured actual human women made of flesh and blood, plus an estimated average of 34 pounds of silicone apiece. There was one woman walking around accompanied by the largest pair of breasts I personally have ever seen. Any given one of these breasts would, in most cities, require a zoning variance.

But the weird thing was, the badge-wearing guys seemed to be less interested in the real women than in the computerized women. At the first booth I came to, a small crowd had gathered to watch a guy operate a CD-ROM[4] computer game wherein the goal was to get the woman on the screen (most of these games feature video footage of women) to undress. The man, using the mouse, clicked on the woman's various body parts; if he clicked on the right part, the woman would say things like "Oh YES!" and remove some item of clothing, but if he clicked on the wrong part, she'd say, "What kind of girl do you think I *am*?"—and the game

4. "CD-ROM" is a group of initials.

would be over. The crowd watched solemnly as the guy clicked away, trying to get the woman to take off her brassiere. He was frowning with concentration, looking for all the world as though he were performing a particularly tricky type of brain surgery.

I don't want to get too heavily philosophical here, but the sad truth is that this game perfectly reveals how a lot of guys wish that sexual relationships really worked: You'd just click in the right place, and: Bingo! Score! No need for all that . . . *talking*.

A few steps away was an exhibitor offering a chance to see a new 3-D computer sex game. There was a line of serious-looking, badge-wearing guys waiting to get into a little enclosed booth; from inside the booth came the recorded sounds of women in the throes of feigned orgasmic passion: "Oh oh oh ah ah AHH AHHHH YES YES YES *YES YES YESSSSSS* . . ." etc. I didn't go in the booth, so I don't know what the specific cause of the moaning was. Perhaps the women had just discovered an exciting new function of the Windows 95© Taskbar.

A few yards away I overheard a conversation between two serious-looking, suit-wearing exhibitors, apparently talking about some new product.

"Are they X-rated, or what?" one of them said.

"They're really dancing on the line," said the other. "I mean, I definitely saw insertion."

At another booth I watched as an extremely nerdy exhibitor—I'm talking about a guy who makes Bill Gates look like Brad Pitt—enthusiastically demonstrated a CD-ROM program to a businessman with a foreign accent. This program allowed you to "direct" your own porno movie; you'd pick the kind of scenes you wanted, and the computer would somehow splice them together.

"OK," said the nerd, moving his computer mouse around the screen, very proud of this program, talking about it the way you'd talk about a new word processor. "You go to your menu here, and you can pick anything you want—Regular Sex; Three-Way; Pussy-Eating; Anal; Anal with Dildo; whatever."

To illustrate his point, he clicked on the "Anal with Dildo" menu item, and sure enough, there it was, on the screen, anal with dildo, in color. The foreign businessman looked impressed.

"This is new frontier," he said.

Indeed it is. And from the looks of things at AdultDex, it's only the beginning; as the hardware and software[5] continue to evolve, this fast-growing billion-dollar industry will undoubtedly come up with newer and better ways to help losers whack off. And to think that just a few decades ago there was nothing but *National Geographic*!

Yes, a brighter day is indeed dawning; that is what I was thinking as I left AdultDex and began the Death March back to the Total Lack of Quality Inn. Whether we're ready or not, computers are rapidly changing our

COMDEX

5. Insert your own clever "hardware" and "software" double entendres here.

lives in every area—not just smut, but also business, communications, medicine, education, government, and sucking androids through fans. The people at Comdex are on the cutting edge of this change; their ideas, their products, and their visions have the potential to make the world a very different place for the rest of us. So it's probably just as well that, what with the taxi situation, most of them will never make it back to the airport.

6.
SOFTWARE

Making Your Computer Come Alive So It Can Attack You

O nce you've determined what kind of computer you need,[1] you must decide what kind of software to run on it. Without software, a computer is just a lump of plastic; whereas *with* software, it's a lump of plastic that can permanently destroy critical data.

What is software? Really, it's nothing more than a series of instructions—called a program—that a computer follows. For example, the program that controls your bank's ATM machine probably looks something like this:

1. DISPLAY MESSAGE: "WELCOME TO INTELLI-TELLER! PLEASE INSERT CARD."
2. UPON CARD INSERTION, DISPLAY MESSAGE: "PLEASE ENTER PASSWORD AND PRESS ENTER."

---

1. Answer: Some computer other than the one you actually have.

---

3. AFTER CUSTOMER ENTERS PASSWORD AND PRESSES ENTER, WAIT 45 SECONDS, THEN DISPLAY MESSAGE: "WELCOME TO INTELLI-TELLER! PLEASE INSERT CARD."
4. WHEN CUSTOMER HAS PUSHED EVERY BUTTON 50 TIMES AND HAS FOREHEAD VEINS THROBBING LIKE CRAZED BAIT, DISPLAY MESSAGE: "THANK YOU FOR USING INTELLI-TELLER! HAVE A NICE DAY!"
5. SEND CARD TO CARD-MELTER.

Of course this is an extremely simple program; modern software is capable of handling far more complex tasks. In fact, as the "brains" of your computer, software has become so "smart" that it can perform many of the functions that *your* brain performs, including gathering information, weighing options, making decisions, getting nervous, lying, forgetting where you left the car keys, and fantasizing about addressing an Amway convention naked.

In fact, modern software has become so sophisticated that it can actually "think" as well as human beings—and perhaps even better. This was proven beyond any doubt in the historic series of chess matches played between world champion Garry Kasparov and an IBM supercomputer named "Deep Blue."[2] The series came down to one final game, and

---

2. Although the other chess-playing computers, when they are hanging out in the locker room, call it by its jocular nickname, "RPX503949632343546."

Kasparov, displaying the brilliantly unconventional attacking strategy that most experts thought would give him an insurmountable advantage over any machine, appeared to have it won. But Deep Blue—which is capable of analyzing 200 million possible moves per *second*—pondered what appeared to be a hopeless situation, and then, in one of the most dramatic reversals in the history of chess, sent an estimated 45,000 volts of electricity into Kasparov's body. Unethical, you say? A flagrant violation of the rules? Fine: Let's see *you* explain that to Deep Blue, who by the way has branched out to other games and is now also the undisputed World Champion in checkers, Monopoly, Chutes and Ladders, arm-wrestling, and Tickle Bee.

Fortunately, you probably will not have to deal with software at this level of sophistication. But you will have to learn how to install and attempt to use it. So let's review the Software Basics, starting with:

WHAT KIND OF SOFTWARE YOU NEED

First off, you need an *operating system*, which is the "Godfather" program that operates behind the scenes, telling all the other programs what to do, making sure they cooperate, and if necessary leaving the heads of virtual horses in their beds. The most popular operating system in world history as of 10:30 A.M. today is Windows 95©, but there are many other options, including Windows 3.1©, Windows 3.11©, Windows 3.111©, Windows for Workgroups©, Windows for Groups That Mainly Just Screw Around©, Windows for Repeat Offenders©, Lo-Fat Windows©, and The Artist Formerly Known As Windows©. There is also the old MS-DOS operating system, which is actually written on parchment and is rarely used on computers manufactured after the French and Indian War. And there is OS/2, which was developed at enormous expense by IBM and marketed as a Windows alternative, and which has won a loyal following of thousands of people, an estimated three of whom do not work for IBM. And of course there is the Apple operating system, or "Apple operating system," for your hippie beatnik weirdo loner narcotics-ingesting communistic types of Apple-owning individuals who are frankly too wussy to handle the challenge of hand-to-hand combat with computer systems specifically designed to thwart them.

So there are many different operating systems available, each with different capabilities, advantages, and drawbacks. Which one is right for your specific needs? The answer is: *Whichever one is already on your computer.* Believe me, you do *not* want to try to install a new operating system yourself. I have done this several times, and it is terrifying. Your computer is taken over by an Evil Demon Installation Program, very much the way the young Linda Blair was taken over in the movie *The Exorcist.* First your screen goes blank, and then suddenly your computer starts asking you a series of questions that you could never answer in a million years, like:

The Installation Program has determined that a conflict exists between your IRQ Port Parameter Module and your Cache Initialization Valve. Shall the Installation Program reallocate the Motherboard Transfer Polarity Replication Allotment, or shall it adjust the Disk Controller Impedance Threshold? Bear in mind that if you answer this question incorrectly, all of your data will be lost and innocent people could die.

And:

Before it will proceed any further with the installation, the Installation Program wishes you to name the capital of Cameroon.

And:

How many men are in your unit? What is your objective? What is your radio frequency? What is the password? ANSWER! THE INSTALLATION PROGRAM HAS WAYS TO MAKE YOU TALK!

This can go on for many hours, and at any moment your computer may start laughing in a diabolical manner and spinning its monitor around 360 degrees and projectile-vomiting green stuff.[3]

I remember a couple of years ago when my son, Rob, in an act of great bravery, attempted to install the "OS/2" operating system, which came in the form of about 8,000 diskettes accompanied by a manual the size of a Toyota Camry. The computer was working fine when Rob started; after several hours of installation, it was a totally dysfunctional, muttering, potentially violent thing, and we had to take it outside and shoot it.[4]

So the bottom line is, you should stick with the operating system you have now. But there are many other exciting programs that you can put on your computer's hard drive. As you're deciding which ones you want, always remember that the ultimate purpose of all software is to provide you with a sufficient level of computing power so that your hard drive gets filled up and you need to buy a new computer.

Here are some of the basic programs that everybody should have:

A Word Processor.[5]   There are many excellent word processors available, including Word, WordPerfect,

---

3. Your newer multimedia computers vomit in a variety of colors.
4. Actually, since this happened in Miami, all we really had to do was take it outside, where passing motorists shot it.
5. See chapter 8 for more information on how you can use word processing to make your ordinary-looking documents much longer.

WordBarelyAdequate, BigWord, BadWord, and Wurd-ForNonspellers. You should get a "full-featured" word processor, defined as "a word processor that has thousands of functions that you will never have any conceivable use for." A good rule of thumb is: If it takes you about three weeks of practicing eight hours a day before you can successfully type and print out a simple sentence, then you have a "full-featured" word processor.

Also, it goes without saying that *any* word processor you purchase—and here I speak on behalf of literally tens of thousands of experienced writing professionals—*must* be able to make a line of italic squirrels.[6]

A Scheduling Program.　You know how annoying it can be to keep a schedule on old-fashioned paper: Every time you want to record an appointment, you have to get out your schedule book and write the appointment down. Wouldn't it be easier if you simply had to go to your computer, turn it on, wait for it to "boot up," use the mouse to locate and click on the scheduling-program icon, wait for the program to load, then use the mouse to get to the right day, then type in the appointment information in the proper space, and the time in the proper space, making sure to use the format allowed by the program, then close the scheduling

---

6. "Italic Squirrels" would be a great name for a rock band.

program without being 100 percent certain that you would ever see this information again?

If you answered "Yes!" then you're ready to join the millions of cyberhumans like me who have dumped clumsy schedule-and-address books weighing as much as three ounces and are now carrying around laptop computers that can incorporate the same information in a package that—including power cables, spare batteries, etc.—weighs easily 25 times as much! It's only a matter of time before we start writing our grocery lists on our laptops and carrying them with us around the supermarket. We don't care what you think. We *love* our laptops.

A Personal Finance Program. Did you know that your computer can handle your personal finances? Well, it can! You can buy the hugely popular program called Quicken, install it on your computer, and within a matter of just minutes you'll be entering your financial records! Figure on about a year for this.

But it's well worth the effort, because once everything is entered, Quicken can take over the job of managing your money: It can balance your checkbook, manage your investments, do your taxes—even pay your bills automatically via electronic banking transfers! You don't even have to know what's going on! You can be *totally oblivious* to what's happening to your money, all thanks to a program written by people you don't even know, people who could probably figure out a clever way to have their program transfer your money into *their* accounts if they wanted to! I bet they could even figure out a way to have their program monitor the *other* programs on your computer, so that if, for example, you were using your word processor to write something negative about Quicken, it could take over your keyboard and

> **PAY NO ATTENTION TO WHAT MR. BARRY IS WRITING ABOUT QUICKEN. QUICKEN IS A GOOD PROGRAM. QUICKEN IS A SAFE PROGRAM. THERE IS NO REASON TO FEAR QUICKEN. YOU LIKE QUICKEN. YOU MUST HAVE QUICKEN. YOU ARE GETTING VERY SLEEPY. YOU WILL BUY QUICKEN.**

Another essential kind of software you need to get is:

A Mindless Game to Play When You're On the Phone. You may have noticed that when you talk on the phone with computer users, you don't seem to have their full attention. This is because they're playing some kind of game, usually solitaire, which comes preloaded on many computer systems. Solitaire is a phenomenally stupid and pointless game, so naturally computer users become obsessed with winning at it, to the exclusion of almost all other concerns. This is why they sound the way they do over the phone.

You: Bob, you remember when you did the cooling-system specs for the Weasel Point power plant?

Bob: Yeah, I, hmmm . . . *Yes!* Black 6!

You: Bob? The Weasel Point plant?

Bob: The what?

You: *Listen*, Bob! The Weasel Point reactor is over-heating badly and they can't control it and you need to . . .

Bob: Hey, there's *two* red queens, right? So where the hell is the other one?

You: Bob, for God's sake, you need to get down there *right now* because in about two hours the whole thing's gonna . . .

Bob: Get down where?

Yes, a mindless game will definitely help you pass the time at work while at the same time benefiting society by preventing the Gross National Product from becoming unnecessarily large.

Another indispensable software tool for anybody who cares about the important political and social issues of the day is:

An Anagram Generator. I don't wish to toot my own journalistic horn, but many observers believe that the turning point in the 1992 race for the Democratic presidential nomination was when I broke the story during the New Hampshire primary that the letters in "Paul E. Tsongas" could be rearranged to spell "GASEOUS PLANT." I believe I was also the first journalist to reveal that "Arlen Specter" can be rearranged to spell "CREEP RENTALS," and that

"Winston Churchill" can be rearranged to spell "HURLS COW CHIN LINT."

How do I obtain this kind of vital information? I use an anagram-generating program. I simply type in a name or phrase, and in a few seconds my computer spews out a list of all the things that it can be rearranged to spell. For example, just now I typed in "Regis Philbin" and found that it could be rearranged to spell, among many other things, "GLIB IRISH PEN" and "NIP HIS GERBIL." This task took me maybe a minute —a stark contrast to the way anagrams were generated back in the days of George Washington, who, lacking computer power, used teams of slaves to determine, after months of grueling labor, that his name could be rearranged to spell "I GNAW HOG ESTROGEN."

Of course there are those who believe that the old, manual system of making anagrams is better; that computers lack the flair and imagination to develop a truly *great* anagram. One person who feels this way is my good friend Gene Weingarten, an editor at the *Washington Post* who does all his anagrams manually. To say that Gene is "serious" about his anagram work is like saying that the Pacific Ocean is "damp." But Gene gets results: He is widely credited with being the first person to discover that "H. Ross Perot" can be rearranged to spell "SHORT POSER."

So I figured that Gene would be the perfect human to use for a Human *vs.* Machine anagram-generating competition, similar to the Big Blue *vs.* Garry Kasparov chess battle, but with lower voltage. I called Gene, and he instantly agreed to set aside his career and family for as long as it took to engage in this competition. We agreed that the name we'd generate anagrams from would be: William Gates.

I hung up the phone and typed "William Gates" into my computer. In less than 90 seconds, it had generated *10,095 anagrams*. Of course most of them were terrible ("I WAG ILL MEATS"), but I thought some of them were OK.

I didn't hear from Gene for several days, during which I do not believe he slept. Then he got back to me, and, after complaining that WILLIAM GATES is a lousy set of letters, he read me his list of anagrams, which I'll show you next to the ones I culled from my computer list:

Anagrams Generated By Gene Weingarten	Anagrams Generated By My Computer
IS WALLET MAGI	I AM GILL SWEAT
I'LL SMITE A WAG	SALAMI WIGLET
WILL I TAME GAS?	I'LL AIM WET GAS
G, I WASTE A MILL	TAIL-WAG SLIME
IGA SWILL MEAT	I MATE ALL WIGS
AT MILLI-WAGES	ALIAS "ELM TWIG"
WILT'S L.A. IMAGE	EMITS GAL WAIL
I WILL EAT GAMS	SLIM ALGAE WIT
I, ALL-WIT GAMES	I AM A SWELL GIT
A WILT-GASM LIE	I SWIG MALT ALE

When we look at these two lists, we are forced to conclude that, although the computer is very fast, it would never have come up with the concept of a "wilt-gasm." To be honest, I had no idea what a "wilt-gasm" *was* until Gene explained it to me.

"It's a *Wilt Chamberlain orgasm*," he said in an irritated voice. "It's *very funny*. Just *accept* that."

"Yes!" I hastily agreed. "VERY funny! Ha ha! Get some sleep!"

So we see that the human brain *can* compete with a computer, but the human pays a tragic price in terms of marble loss. It's better to just get an anagram-generating program; or, if you insist on the "human touch," call Gene Weingarten at the *Washington Post*, a newspaper that has earned the respect of the world journalism community because *"Washington Post"* can be rearranged to spell "WANT SPIGOTS, HON?" as well as "SH! PAWNS TOOTING!"[7]

OK, we've covered almost all of your basic software needs. There are just a couple more programs that everybody should have, including:

A Home Lawyer Program. Let's face it, in these lawsuit-intensive times, you really should have a lawyer advising you in every transaction, no matter how minor. Suppose you ask a co-worker for a stick of chewing gum. If you just accept the gum, with no legal agreement spelling out the conditions of the

---

7. Not to mention: TOWN GASP: "NO SHIT!"

transfer, you have no protection if this co-worker should at some point down the road claim that he did not intend to *give* you this stick of gum, only *lend* it. You could wind up in court without a leg to stand on!

So you need legal advice, but you can't afford to pay the kind of hefty legal fees that your top-quality lawyers must charge to compensate themselves for the brain strain involved in thinking up sentences containing large scary words such as "therein," "aforementioned," "quid pro quo," and "delicatessen."

What can you do? You can do what I did, which is go to the Bargain Software Bin of your computer store and purchase, for under $10, a home lawyer program. Mine is called "Do-It-Yourself Lawyer," and according to the box it has "Over 65 E-Z Legal Forms . . . Quickly Create *Ironclad Legal Documents* in the Privacy of Your Own Home!"

I used Do-It-Yourself Lawyer to create an ironclad legal document covering the hypothetical chewing-gum transfer. The program asked me a few simple questions about names and addresses, then produced the following document:

GENERAL ASSIGNMENT

BE IT KNOWN, for value received, the undersigned L. Fenton Wingle of West Fromage, Arkansas, hereby unconditionally and irrevocably assigns and transfers unto Walter A. "The Clam" Plinkett of South Fromage, Arkansas, all right, title and interest in and to the following: one (1) stick of Juicy Fruit brand chewing gum, unchewed, in the original wrapper.

The undersigned fully warrants that it has full rights and authority to enter into this assignment and that the rights and benefits assigned hereunder are free and clear of any lien, encumbrance, adverse claim, or interest by any third party.

This assignment shall be binding upon and inure to the benefit of the parties, and their successors and assigns.

Signed this 8th day of October, 1996.

_____

Assignor

_____

Assignee

Isn't that great? Doesn't it just look so . . . *legal?* It even has a "hereunder" in it! Talk about ironclad! You can just imagine the bond of trust that will develop between you and your co-worker when you insist that he sign this document before you will accept his gum.

Frankly, now that we have software like this, I don't see why anybody needs to go to law school anymore. You remember that laptop computer that Judge Lance Ito[8] always had in front of him during the O.J. Simpson trial? It wouldn't surprise me to learn that he had Do-It-Yourself Lawyer running on there, giving him instructions (**"CALL A RECESS! YOU HAVE SOMETHING STICKING OUT OF YOUR NOSE!"**). The way software is developing, it's only a matter of time before we have Do-It-Yourself Dentist, Do-It-Yourself Commercial Airline Pilot, and Do-It-Yourself Surgeon (**"AFTER WASHING HANDS, PICK UP SCALPEL. NOTE: IF HAND BLEEDS, PICK UP SCALPEL BY OTHER END."**).

OK, now we've covered all of your fundamental software needs except for one, and I bet you know which one! That's right: You are not really getting maximum personal productivity with your computer unless you have . . .

A SIMULATED BASS-FISHING PROGRAM. As I've grown older, I've noticed that I never go fishing

---

8. JUDGE LANCE ITO = NO GET JUICE, LAD

anymore. I've spent a lot of time pondering why this is, and I've finally reached the conclusion that it's because I hate fishing. I mean, you sit out in an unstable boat on an algae-encrusted, rank-smelling lake wearing a big invisible sign that says ☞EAT ME☜ in mosquito language, and you impale yourself on nasty little hooks, and you spend hours trying to outwit an animal with the IQ of ketchup, and then if you finally accomplish your objective, you wind up with this . . . this *fish*, lying there in your boat, gasping, dying slowly, staring at you with whichever eyeball is on your side, and you can almost hear it saying to you, in a gasping but very sarcastic fish voice, "Well, I hope that was fun for *you*, Mr. Sportsperson."

Who needs that? Not me, which is why I stopped fishing—until I discovered simulated-fishing programs, which I swear I am not making up. Mine is called "Trophy Bass," and it starts by creating a virtual lake on my computer screen, featuring the sounds of virtual birds, crickets, frogs, etc., chirping and peeping out of my speaker. Then I navigate my little virtual motorboat around the lake, accompanied by the Virtual Fishing Guide. He's in a little box in the corner of the screen, wearing a baseball-style cap. He appears to have no body; he's just a head. When I click on his face, he gives me helpful tips like: "There should be fish here!"

Then I select a virtual lure, cast it with my virtual rod, and . . . YES! The **"FISH ON"** sign flashes, and I am battling a thrashing lunker,[9] using all my mouse skills, while the computer plays peppy sporting music. Then finally I get the fish, and my screen displays a detailed color picture of it, plus how much it weighs. It's a very gratifying moment; I would exchange high-fives with the Virtual Fishing Guide, if only he had arms.

You can call me an ecology nut if you want, but I always let the fish go.

Anyway, we have now covered all the basic types of software that every computer owner should have. To review, you need, in addition to your simulated bass-fishing program: a word processor; a calendar program; a mindless game to play when you should be working; an anagram generator; a home lawyer program; and a personal finance program such as Quicken or

> **THERE IS NO PERSONAL FINANCE PROGRAM OTHER THAN QUICKEN. THERE IS ONLY QUICKEN. YOU LOVE QUICKEN. QUICKEN IS GOD. YOU WILL BUY QUICKEN.**

9. Whatever that means.

7.
HOW TO INSTALL SOFTWARE

A 12-Step Program

1. Examine the software packaging until you find a little printed box that explains what kind of computer system you need to run the software. It should look something like this:

SYSTEM REQUIREMENTS
2386 PROCESSOR OR HIGHER
628.8 MEGAHERTZ MODEM
719.7 MB FREE DISK SPACE
3546 MB RAM
432323 MB ROM
05948737 MB RPM
ANTILOCK BRAKING SYSTEM
2 TURTLE DOVES

NOTE: This software will not work on your computer.

---

2. Open the software packaging and remove the manual. This will contain detailed instructions on installing, operating, and troubleshooting the software. Throw it away.

3. Find the actual software, which should be in the form of either a 3.5-inch floppy diskette or a CD-ROM, located inside a sealed envelope that says:

LICENSING AGREEMENT

By breaking this seal, the user hereinafter agrees to abide by all the terms and conditions of the following agreement that nobody ever reads, as well as the Geneva Convention and the U.N. Charter and the Secret Membership Oath of the Benevolent Protective Order of the Elks and such other terms and conditions, real and imaginary, as the Software Company shall deem necessary and appropriate, including the right to come to the user's home and examine the user's hard drive, as well as the user's underwear drawer if we feel like it, take it or leave it, until death do us part, one nation indivisible, by the dawn's early light, in the name of the Father, the Son, and the Holy Ghost, finders keepers, losers weepers, thanks you've been a great crowd, and don't forget to tip your servers.

---

4. Hand the software to a child aged 3 through 12 and say, "(Name of child), please install this on my computer."

5. If you have no child aged 3 through 12, insert the software in the appropriate drive, type "SETUP" and press the Enter key.

6. Turn the computer on, you idiot.

7. Once again type "SETUP" and press the Enter key.

8. You will hear grinding and whirring noises[1] for a while, after which the following message should appear on your screen:

> The Installation Program will now examine your system to see what would be the best way to render it inoperable. Is that OK with you? Choose one, and be honest:

YES	SURE

9. After you make your selection, you will hear grinding and whirring for a very long time while the installation program does God knows what in there. Some installation programs can actually alter molecular structures, so that when they're done, your computer has been transformed into an entirely new device, such as a food processor. At the very least, the installation program will create many new directories, sub-directories and sub-sub-directories on your hard drive and fill them with thousands of mysterious files with names like "puree.exe," "fester.dat," and "doo.wah."

---

1. These are caused by the Whirring Grinding Unit, or WGU.

10. When the installation program is finished, your screen should display the following message:

> ### CONGRATULATIONS
> The installation program cannot think of anything else to do to your computer and has grown bored. You may now attempt to run your software. If you experience any problems, electrical shocks, insomnia, shortness of breath, nasal discharge, or intestinal parasites, you should immediately

11. At this point your computer system should become less functional than the federal government, refusing to respond even when struck with furniture.

12. Call the toll-free Technical Support Hotline number listed on the package and wait on the line for a representative, who will explain to you, in a clear, step-by-step manner, how to adopt a child aged 3 through 12.

8.
WORD PROCESSING

How to Press an Enormous Number of Keys Without Ever Actually Writing Anything

OR

If God Had Wanted Us to Be Concise, He Wouldn't Have Given Us So Many Fonts

Not that I am recommending this, but if you were to sit down and actually *read* some of the so-called great writers of the past, you would notice immediately that, most of the time, they make no sense whatsoever. Take William Shakespeare, who was a famous writer during the Shakespearean Era.[1] Most of his material looks, to the naked eye, like this:

1. This occurred in the past.

Hamlet: O did'st thine vesper'd dreams 'ere brunt the day?

Nor can'st thou find'st not plums in frinkle-whey?

Gertrude: *What?*

It goes on like this for scene after scene, act after act, until finally the main characters, driven insane by the fact that they're all speaking gibberish, kill themselves.

What was Shakespeare's problem? How could a person produce so much writing—38 plays, 157 sonnets, 2 major narrative poems, and 8 screenplays—and not manage to produce more than four sentences, total, that a normal person can understand?

The answer is that Shakespeare did not have word processing. He had to write everything out by hand, and, like most people, his handwriting was almost totally illegible. The actors in his plays were forced to guess what their lines were, and by the time the words got into print, they had almost nothing to do with what Shakespeare originally wrote (for example, *Hamlet* was supposed to be a comedy about a man who marries a camel).

And the problem is not limited to Shakespeare. Even today, hardly anybody can read anybody else's handwriting. Oh, sure, we all start *out* writing legibly, in elementary school, when we have to write on that special writing paper with the lines really far apart, so that a capital "A" is approximately the height of

Danny DeVito. Also, we learn to *print*, and the teachers force us to form each letter clearly and legibly, like this:

"Oh oh oh," said Jane. "Look look look. Spot made a big doot."

Thanks to the Great Big Printing Method, until we reach about age 8, we all write legibly. Then the schools—in what I believe is the single biggest impediment to human productivity—teach us all how to write in script, or "cursive." Nobody knows why the schools do this; it's one of those inexplicable traditions that we observe without knowing why, like changing the clocks for Daylight Saving Time.

Whatever the reason, cursive is a terrible idea. The very word is Latin for "a kind of handwriting that is legible only to the person who is writing it." Oh, sure, cursive looks OK when we're first learning it, and the teachers are making us write nice, clear letters:

Spot made a big doot.

But as soon as we get out of the classroom our handwriting starts to degenerate, and pretty soon it has mutated into a series of random marks, as can be seen in the following example:

TYPICAL EXAMPLE OF "CURSIVE" HANDWRITING. This is an actual photographic close-up of a note written by President Harry S Truman on August 3, 1945. Truman later revealed that the purpose of the note was to request waffles for breakfast, although at the time his staff interpreted it to mean "Let's drop the atomic bomb."

The result of the cursive training is that only about 75 adults in the United States have legible handwriting, and all of these adults are elementary-school teachers. I know what I'm talking about here. As a newspaper columnist, I get a lot of handwritten fan mail, and much of it is unreadable. Granted, this is partly because a lot of my fans wear special restraining devices and have to hold their writing implements in their teeth. But even the relatively normal ones write in such a way that I can decipher only the occasional word, so that most of my fan mail reads like this:

Mr. Barry:
Cancel (SOMETHING) *subscription, you* (SOMETHING). (SOMETHING) (SOMETHING) *idiot.* (SOMETHING) "*humor*" (SOMETHING) (SOMETHING) *dangerous!* (SOMETHING) (SOMETHING) (SOMETHING) *8-year-old* (SOMETHING) (SOMETHING) *your article* (SOMETHING) (SOMETHING) (SOMETHING)

swallowed an entire **(SOMETHING)**
(SOMETHING) *chemicals!* **(SOMETHING)**
(SOMETHING) (SOMETHING) (SOMETHING)
surgery **(SOMETHING) (SOMETHING)** *artificial*
pelvis. **(SOMETHING) (SOMETHING)** *my*
lawyer. **(SOMETHING)** *you!*

Because I can't understand my mail, I am forced to respond in vague terms ("**(SOMETHING)** *you, too!* "), and all hope of real communication is lost.

But the repercussions of the handwriting problem extend far beyond professional writers such as me and William Shakespeare. Have you ever asked yourself why the federal government, despite employing millions of bright people, displays the collective intelligence of a squeegee? The answer is that all of the important early documents that our government is based on—the Constitution, the Declaration of Independence, the Magna Carta, and the Scarlet Letter—are written in totally illegible cursive handwriting. For over 200 years the Supreme Court has been basically guessing what the Constitution says. It is only recently that historians, using modern handwriting-analysis equipment, have been able to start deciphering the handwriting; so far they have discovered that:

- The so-called Bill of Rights is actually a detailed order for party supplies.
- There's no mention of any "Congress."

■ The president *is* mentioned, but his only specified duty—which is not further explained—is to "blow the Horn of Cheese."

I could go on and on with historical examples of the handwriting problem. You would be shocked if I were to tell you the original title of what is now referred to as the "Old Testament."[2] Suffice it to say that handwriting has been confusing humanity in general, and the medical profession[3] in particular, for thousands of years.

Things improved slightly in 1873,[4] when the typewriter was invented. The big advantage of the typewriter was that it produced clear, legible words; the drawback was that the standard keyboard, which we still use today, was invented by dyslexics from Mars, so that the letters you need a lot, such as "o," are hard to find and sometimes missing entirely; whereas totally unnecessary letters such as "q" appear as many as four times apiece. To make matters worse, many people type by the Forefinger Lunge method, which means they make a lot of mistakes, which in turn means that they have to do a lot of crossing out, so that reading their documents is like listening to Porky Pig try to complete a sentence:

2. "Basic Sandal Repair."
3. For example, a recent study showed that in 1995, 78 percent of all unnecessary organ removals resulted from hospital personnel misinterpreting notes scribbled by doctors who were in most cases merely reminding themselves that it was time to purchase a new Lexus.
4. Or whenever the hell the typewriter was invented.

~~Dew~~ ~~Deqr~~ Dear ~~Mt.~~ Mr. ~~Fwr~~ Freebit:
~~Regq~~ ~~Regatg~~ ~~Regarsng~~ About ~~tge~~ the ~~Snicklemab~~
Spinkleman ~~Spock~~ ~~Spee~~ ~~Sprocle~~ Sprocket ~~cob~~
~~contrav~~ ~~contrq~~ contract, ~~teh~~ the ~~spr~~ ~~s{p~~ ~~specofi~~
~~specifiva~~ ~~specificatipns~~ numbers ~~arw~~ are
~~incorect~~ ~~inccor~~ ~~imco~~ ~~shit~~ call me about ~~thid~~ this.
~~Sincert~~ Sincerely,
~~Robwr~~ ~~Roner~~ ~~Ribrt~~ Bob

But everything is different and wonderful now, because now we have—get ready for 36-point type in the "Playbill" font surrounded by a double-lined 2¼-point box with shading—

WORD PROCESSING

Modern computerized word processing enables us, both as individuals and as a cohesive societal entity, to exponentially enhance and aggrandize the parameters, both qualitative and quantitative, not to mention paradigmatic, of our communicative conceptualizations because now we can spell great big words correctly without having a clue what they mean. This is made possible thanks to "spell-checking," which is when the computer goes through your writing, finds your mistakes, and shows you exactly how to fix them. For example, suppose you're trying to win the business of a major prospective client, and you write him the following letter:

> **Deer Mr. Strompel:**
> **It was a grate pleasure too meat you're**
> **staff, and the undersigned look foreword**
> **too sea you soon inn the near future.**

Clearly, you would not create a very good impression with a letter like this. But thanks to modern computerized word processing, you have nothing to worry about. Because when you use your spell-checker on this letter, not only does it inform you that there is no such word as "Strompel," but it also *suggests the word that you probably meant to use.* It can even make the substitution for you! The result is that your prospective client sees the following impressive document:

> **Deer Mr. Strumpet:**
> **It was a grate pleasure too meat you're**
> **staff, and the undersigned look foreword**
> **too sea you soon inn the near future.**

But spell-checking is just one of the advantages of modern computerized word processing. There is also an extremely helpful feature called "grammar-checking," which, when I apply it to the preceding sentence, informs me that it is preferable not to start a sentence with "but." It also informs me that the preceding sentence has a Flesch Reading Ease score of 44.0; a Flesch-Kincaid Grade Level of 10.4; a Coleman-Liau Grade Level of 15.9; and a Bormuth Grade Level of 11.1. I have no idea what these numbers mean, but I assume you're supposed to use them to tailor your writing to your specific reader's mental capabilities, assuming you can find out what they are ("Deer Mr. Strumpet: Please inform the undersigned of you're Coleman-Liau Grade Level").

Another truly wonderful thing you can do with modern computerized word processing is "copy and paste." This makes it easy to copy something and repeat it as many times as you want to without retyping it. This makes it easy to copy something and repeat it as many times as you want to without retyping it. This makes it easy to copy something and repeat it as many times as you want to without retyping it. This makes it easy to copy something and repeat it as many times as you want to without retyping it. It's *easy*, thanks to "copy and paste"!

You can use this capability to make any document much longer without having to personally think of anything to say. As you can imagine, this is a tremendous help to students who have been assigned to write research papers of a certain minimum length. This is now absurdly easy, especially if your computer has a CD-ROM drive, which enables you to copy huge gobs of information off CD-ROM disks and stick them anywhere you want.

For example, I have a CD-ROM disk called the

Microsoft© Bookshelf☺, which includes—all on one disk—a dictionary, an abridged encyclopedia, a thesaurus, an almanac, a book of famous quotations, a chronology of historical events, a world atlas, and a ZIP code directory. Now suppose that I am a high school student, and it's 11 P.M. on a Sunday night, and I just remembered that four weeks ago I was assigned to write a 3,000-word report, which is due tomorrow morning, on Photosynthesis, which I know absolutely nothing about because nobody ever mentions it on MTV. In the old days, I would have been forced to spend hours copying information manually from the encyclopedia, but now, all I have to do is fire up my CD-ROM, and within a few minutes I have cranked out the following scholarly document:

PHOTOSYNTHESIS[5]

In any discussion of a topic such as photosynthesis, it is important—in the sense of "crucial, critical, key, momentous, climactic, pivotal, and decisive"—to ask the question: "What is photosynthesis?" The dictionary definition, of course, is:

pho·to·syn·the·sis (fo′to-sîn¹thî–sîs) *noun* – The process in green plants and certain other organisms by which carbohydrates are synthesized from carbon

---

5. Just about every word in the following report was stolen directly from various major publishers represented in the Microsoft Bookshelf, and if you try to use any of these words without their permission, or even *read* some of these words, packs of carnivorous lawyers will come around to your place of residence and explain the situation until your ears bleed.

dioxide and water using light as an energy source. Most forms of photosynthesis release oxygen as a byproduct.

We deduce from this definition that photosynthesis is, basically, a noun describing the process in green plants and certain other organisms by which carbohydrates are synthesized from carbon dioxide and water using light as an energy source. But this definition, in and of itself, is not enough for a truly *scientific* discussion of this topic at a depth of 3,000 words (139 to this point).

For when we use the word "scientific," we are reminded of the famous quotation first emitted by **Leo Tolstoy** (1828–1910), the famous Russian novelist and philosopher, who, in chapter 10 of the book *What Is Art?* (1898; repr. in *Tolstoy on Art,* ed. by Aylmer Maude, 1924), is quoted on the subject of science as follows: "True science investigates and brings to human perception such truths and such knowledge as the people of a given time and society consider most important. Art transmits these truths from the region of perception to the region of emotion."

What, exactly, did Tolstoy, the famous Russian novelist and philosopher, mean by this? Was he referring to photosynthesis? For that matter, had photosynthesis even been *invented* during the era (1828–1910) in which the famous Russian novelist and philosopher Leo Tolstoy lived? For this was, indeed, an era during which many things occurred. For example, the technical processes and managerial innovations of the English industrial revolution spread to Europe (especially Germany) and the U.S., causing an explosion of industrial production, demand for raw materials, and competition for markets. Inventors, both trained and self-educated, provided the means for larger-scale production (Bessemer steel, 1856; sewing machine, 1846). Many inventions were shown at the 1851 London Great Exhibition at the Crystal Palace, the theme of which was universal prosperity.

But it is also important, as we reach the 372-word mark, not to forget that this was also an era of tragic events such as the American Civil War (1861–65), a conflict between Northern states (UNION) and Southern seceded states (CONFEDERACY). It is known in the South as the War between the States, and by the official Union designation of War of the Rebellion. Many causes over a number of years contributed to what William H. SEWARD called "the irrepressible conflict": sectional rivalry, moral indignation aroused by the ABOLITIONISTS, the question of the extension of slavery into new territories, and a fundamental disagreement about the relative supremacy of federal control or STATES' RIGHTS.

Yet by the same token, the Civil War also produced Abraham Lincoln, who, although he did not specifically mention photosynthesis in his famous Gettysburg Address,[6] which was coincidentally delivered in Gettysburg, Pa. (ZIP codes 17325 and 17326), he did say, quote: "Four score and seven years ago, our fathers brought forth upon this continent a new nation: conceived in liberty, and dedicated to the proposition that . . ."

And so on and so on, great gobs of information gushing out, easy as pie, thanks to CD-ROM and

6. Copyright 1992 Michael Jackson.

"copy and paste." With word processing, there is no end to the amount of words you can crank out without having to become personally involved with what they say. Of course, this is also the basic principle of the computerized form letter, which has become the standard medium of communication sent to humans by organizations, businesses, and government agencies. Most of the letters we receive are generated by computers, using information supplied by other computers, which in turn have gathered it from other computers; the result, as I noted in the Introduction to this book, is that much of the time, the people who send out these letters have no idea what the letters say, or to whom they're being sent.

City of Milwaukee
Department of Codes
Bureau of Rules
Office of Enforcement
Cubicle of No Return

Dear Mr. Dahmer:

It has come to the attention of this department's computer that, while residing in the City of Milwaukee at 924 North 25th St., Apartment 213, you killed people and ate their body parts. Please be advised that this may be a violation of Section 2938.6 of the City of Milwaukee Housing, Zoning and Dining Code, and that you may therefore be subject to certain fines, penalties, and lectures.

Please contact this department immediately by calling the Hotline Number listed below and listening to a recorded voice until your brain turns to guacamole. If you fail to comply, our department's computer will have no choice but to turn your name over to the Motor Vehicle Department's computer, which is so inhuman that it makes our computer look like Andy Griffith.

Sincerely,
L. Fenster LaPlume
Acting Superintendent
Died in 1987 But Still Receiving a
Generous Pension

I should not reveal this, but we in the newspaper medium now produce almost all of our stories via automated word processing. We have found that there is no need to waste time and money having human reporters write entire stories from scratch, when all we really need to do is insert a few current facts into previously written articles:

WASHINGTON—President *(name of president)* charged today that the *(name of congressional committee)* was engaging in a "witch hunt" and using "McCarthy-style tactics" in its investigation of the burgeoning *(name of some insanely complicated, terminally bore-ass scandal)* affair. In response, committee chairman *(name of chairman)* accused the administration of "stonewalling" and pledged to hold hearings "until everybody involved in this matter is dead."

The *(name of scandal)* affair concerns allegations that *(insert standard boilerplate summary of scandal, or insert today's horoscope; it makes no difference, since nobody will ever read this far anyway).*

NEW YORK—The *(name of some organization that sounds authoritative even though nobody ever heard of it, like "Institute of Dietary Fiber")* announced today that a new authoritative study shows that *(name of something that a lot of people consume, such as coffee, Chinese food, celery, or water)*, which only last week had been found by another authoritative study to be *(choose one: "good for you" or "very likely to cause cancer")*, is in fact *(choose one: "very likely to cause cancer" or "good for you")*.

(SOME FOREIGN CITY WITH A NAME LIKE "KZAGBLECH" THAT YOU COULD NOT IN A MILLION YEARS LOCATE ON A MAP)—Fighting resumed today in this war-torn capital following the breakdown of yesterday's cease-fire between *(names of two ethnic groups that have been killing each other nonstop for 6,000 years)*. Deeming the resolution of this conflict "critical to United States interests in *(whatever region this particular conflict is located in),*" President *(name of president)* immediately dispatched U.S. Secretary of State *(name of secretary of state)* to the scene with a suitcase containing five new cease-fire agreements, which, at the current breakage rate of one every 1.7 days, should enable this troubled region to set a new world cease-fire-breaking record by next week.

LOS ANGELES—*(Name of famous male show-business personality)* and *(name of famous female show-business personality)* have announced through a spokesperson that they are splitting up but plan to "continue having illegitimate children."

See how easy it is? Don't tell anybody, but you can even use automated word processing to write newspaper humor columns:

> If you aren't alarmed, then no offense, but you have the intelligence of *(choose one: a peat bog; used chewing gum; gravel; an O.J. Simpson juror)*, because according to an article from the *(name of newspaper)* sent in by alert reader *(name of reader)*, a *(pick one: cow; frog; rutabaga; tax accountant)* recently *(pick one: exploded; fell from the sky; was found in a taco; was found in a toilet; married Donald Trump)*. I am not making this up. Ha ha! Booger.

So to summarize: With word processing, you can produce enormous quantities of correctly spelled words without the time-consuming labor of personally figuring out what they say. This means you can save a lot of time, which is good, because you can use that extra time for a really productive activity—namely, messing around with . . .

Yes!

Once you get into word processing, you'll find that for every minute you spend producing words, you'll spend at least ten minutes deciding what font to put them in. There are hundreds and hundreds of fonts available, and once you start trying out different ones, you discover that it's really **really** **REALLY** hard to stop. This is good, because by creatively using **FONTS**, you can give any document **greater impact.**

Let's take a look at an actual example. Suppose you're a corporate executive writing an important letter to a group of your employees. You don't want to be sending them a document written in some "ho-hum" typeface like this:

Dear Valued Employee:

As you know, this has been a difficult year for all of us, what with the economic recession, combined with the increased foreign competition, combined with . . .

And so on. What a visual snore of a document! Your employees are going to take one look at it and think, "Don't these people have any fonts other than plain old 12-point New Courier?"

Now let's look at how this same letter can be transformed into a high-impact, "must-read" document, thanks to the creative use of fonts:

Dear Valued Employee:

As you know, this has been a DIFFICULT YEAR *for* **ALL** *of us, what with the* ECONOMIC RECESSION, *combined with the increased* FOREIGN COMPETITION, *combined with the unfortunate* **fatal** *oops!* **explosion** *at the Humperville plant, combined with the fact that* ⇒ **OUR** 🏴 **C.E.O.** ⇐ *needs a* **jet** ✈ *with a bigger* **hot tub**. *As a result, we have* **no** **choice** *but to* LET YOU GO 🏃 *effective* Christmas Eve ☹. *But you may* REST ASSURED *that, should our* **future needs** *ever call for employees, we will definitely think about* getting in touch *⌒ with you.*

Warmest Human Seasonal Regards,

Bob Bunderheimer

Human Resources

p.s. Don't forget to turn in your company-owned pencils.

See what a difference a little creativity makes? It makes you wonder what our ancestors could have done if only they had been able to use modern fonts to add "zing" to their writing ("The ☆**LORD**☆ is my **shepherd**; I shall **NOT**⊙ want...")

But that is, frankly, our ancestors' problem. We are extremely fortunate to live in the age of word processing, because, as I noted earlier, you can produce enormous quantities of correctly spelled words without the time-consuming labor of personally figuring out what they say. You can produce enormous quantities of correctly spelled words without the time-consuming labor of personally figuring out what they say. You can produce enormous quantities of correctly spelled words without the time-consuming labor of personally figuring out what they say. You can produce enormous quantities of correctly spelled words without the time-consuming labor of personally figuring out what they say. You can produce enormous quantities of correctly spelled words without the time-consuming labor of personally figuring out what they say. You can produce enormous quantities of correctly spelled words without the time-consuming labor of personally figuring out what they say. You can produce enormous quantities of correctly spelled words without the time-consuming labor of personally figuring out what they say. I think this chapter is plenty long enough now.

9.
THE
INTERNET

Transforming Society and Shaping
the Future, Through Chat

OR

Watch What You Write,
Mr. Chuckletrousers

OR

Why Suck Is OK, Blow Is Not

☞ *PLUS*

Danger! Sushi Tapeworms!

The Internet is the most important single development in the history of human communications
since the invention of "call waiting."

A bold statement? Indeed it is, but consider how the
Internet can simplify and enhance our lives. Imagine
that you need to do the following chores: (1) make an
airline reservation; (2) buy some tickets to a concert;

(3) research a question on your income taxes; and (4) help your child gather information for a school report. To accomplish all this fifteen years ago, you could easily have spent an entire day talking on the phone and driving to the library, IRS office, etc. Whereas today, you simply turn on your computer, dial up your local Internet access number, and in less than an instant—thanks to the Internet's global reach and astounding versatility—you're listening to a busy signal!

Yes, it can be difficult to get through to the Internet, because it's so popular. These days it seems as though *everybody* has one of those cryptic little Internet addresses:

Hunchback@NotreDame.com
jhoffa@landfill.r.i.p
millionsofbacteria@yourarmpit.p-u

Why is the Internet so popular? For one thing, it enables you to communicate quickly and easily with people all over the world—even people you don't *want* to communicate with. I know this for a fact, because one time several years ago, when I was new to the Internet, I attempted to send an electronic message to a writer I know in England named Michael Bywater, whom I met when I was on a book tour in London. Michael and I had really hit it off, in part because we share a common philosophical outlook on important economic, social, and political issues, and in part because we consumed an enormous quantity of beer.

So when I got back to the United States, I wrote Michael this chatty little message, which was basically an inside joke that would make sense only to him. It addressed Michael as "Mr. Chuckletrousers"—a name I'd seen in a London newspaper headline—and it contained various sophisticated and extremely subtle humor elements that could look, to the uninformed observer, like bad words.

The problem was that, because of my limited grasp of how the Internet works, instead of sending this message just to Michael, I somehow managed to send (or, in cyberlingo, "post") it to THE WHOLE ENTIRE INTERNET. It immediately became semi-famous. People called it the Chuckletrousers Post, and it spread like wildfire around the Internet, as people made copies and sent them to their friends, who made copies for *their* friends. As far as I can tell, thousands, perhaps *millions* of people ended up seeing it. To this day, I am regularly approached by total strangers who say, "Hi, Mr. Chuckletrousers!" and then walk off, snickering. If there are in fact intelligent beings elsewhere in the universe, I'm pretty sure that the first communication they will receive from our planet will be the Chuckletrousers Post.[1]

The irony is, about a week after the original post, Michael Bywater—remember him?—posted a message

---

1. If it *is* the first communication they receive, they will immediately vaporize Earth. And they will be right.

on the Internet saying that he'd heard there was some message going around with his name in it, but he hadn't seen it, and could somebody please send it to him? In other words, I had managed to send this hideously embarrassing message to *everybody in the world except the person who was supposed to read it.*

Yes, thanks to the awesome communications capabilities of the Internet, I was able to make an intergalactic fool of myself, and there's no reason why you can't do the same. So get with it! Join the Internet! At first you may be a little confused by some of the jargon, but trust me, after you've spent just a few hours cruising in Cyberspace, you'll be totally lost. To speed this process along, I've prepared the following helpful list of:

COMMON QUESTIONS AND ANSWERS ABOUT THE INTERNET

Q. *What, exactly, is the Internet?*
A. The Internet is a worldwide network of university, government, business, and private computer systems.

Q. *Who runs it?*
A. A 13-year-old named Jason.

Q. *How can I get on the Internet?*
A. The easiest way is to sign up with one of the popular commercial "on-line" services, such as Prodigy,

CompuServe, or America Online, which will give you their program disks for free.[2] Or, if you just leave your house unlocked, they'll sneak in some night and install their programs on your computer when you're sleeping. They *really* want your business.

Q. *What are the benefits of these services?*
A. The major benefit is that they all have simple, "user-friendly" interfaces that enable you—even if you have no previous computer experience—to provide the on-line services with the information they need to automatically put monthly charges on your credit card bill forever.

Q. *What if I die?*
A. They don't care.

Q. *Can't I cancel my account?*
A. Of course! You can cancel your account at any time.

Q. *How?*
A. Nobody has ever been able to find out. Some of us have been trying for *years* to cancel our on-line-service accounts, but no matter what we do, the charges keep appearing on our bills. We're thinking of entering the Federal Witness Protection Program.

---

2. I have received Prodigy disks with *airline peanuts*. Really. They weren't bad, although they could have used a little salt.

Q. *What if I have children?*
A. You'll want an anesthetic, because it *really* hurts.

Q. *No, I mean: What if my children also use my Internet account?*
A. You should just sign your house and major internal organs over to the on-line service right now.

Q. *Aside from running up charges, what else can I do once I'm connected to an on-line service?*
A. Millions of things! An incredible array of things! No end of things!

Q. *Like what?*
A. You can . . . ummmm . . . OK! I have one! You can chat.

Q. *"Chat"?*
A. Chat.

Q. *I can already chat. I chat with my friends.*
A. Yes, but on the Internet, which connects millions of people all over the entire globe, you can chat with *total strangers*, many of whom are boring and stupid!

Q. *Sounds great! How does it work?*
A. Well, first you decide which type of area you wish to chat in. Some areas are just for general chatting, and some are for specific interest groups, such as Teens,

Poets, Cat Lovers, Religious People, Gays, Gay Teens Who Read Religious Poetry to Cats, and of course Guys Having Pointless Arguments About Sports. At any given moment, an area can contain anywhere from two to dozens of people, who use clever fake names such as "ByteMe2" so nobody will know their real identities.

Q. *What are their real identities?*
A. They represent an incredible range of people, people of all ages, in all kinds of fascinating fields—from scientists to singers, from writers to wranglers, from actors to athletes—you could be talking to almost anybody on the Internet!

Q. *Really?*
A. No. You're almost always talking to losers and hormone-crazed 13-year-old boys. But they *pretend* to be writers, wranglers, scientists, singers, etc.

Q. *What do people talk about in chat areas?*
A. Most chat-area discussions revolve around the fascinating topic of who is entering and leaving the chat area. A secondary, but equally fascinating, topic is where everybody lives. Also, for a change of pace, every now and then the discussion is interrupted by a hormone-crazed 13-year-old boy wishing to talk dirty to women.

To give you an idea of how scintillating the repartee can be, here's a re-creation of a typical chat-area dialogue (do not read this scintillating repartee while operating heavy machinery):

LilBrisket: Hi everybody
Wazootyman: Hi LilBrisket
Toadster: Hi Bris
Lungflook: Hi B
LilBrisket: What's going on?
Toadster: Not much
Lungflook: Pretty quiet

(LONGISH PAUSE)

Wazootyman: Anybody here from Texas?
LilBrisket: No
Toadster: Nope
Lungflook: Sorry

(LONGISH PAUSE)

UvulaBob: Hi everybody
Toadster: Hi UvulaBob
Lungflook: Hi Uvula
LilBrisket: Hi UB
Wazootyman: Hi U
UvulaBob: What's happening?
LilBrisket: Kinda slow
Toadster: Same old same old
Lungflook: Pretty quiet
Jason56243837: LilBrisket, take off your panties
LilBrisket: OK, but I'm a man

(LONGISH PAUSE)

Wazootyman: UvulaBob, are you from Texas?
UvulaBob: No.

(LONGISH PAUSE)

Lungflook: Well, gotta run.
Toadster: 'bye, Lungflook
LilBrisket: Take 'er easy, Lungster
Wazootyman: See ya around, Lung
UvulaBob: So long, L

(LONGISH PAUSE)

PolypMaster: Hi everybody
LilBrisket: Hey, PolypMaster
Toadster: Yo, Polyp
UvulaBob: Hi, P
PolypMaster: What's going on?
LilBrisket: Not much
Toadster: Pretty quiet
UvulaBob: Kinda slow . . .

And so it goes in the chat areas, hour after riveting hour, where the ideas flow fast and furious, and at any moment you could learn some fascinating nugget of global-network information, such as whether or not PolypMaster comes from Texas.

Q. *I've heard that people sometimes use Internet chat areas to have "cybersex." What exactly is that?*
A. This is when two people send explicitly steamy messages to each other, back and forth, back and forth,

faster and faster, hotter and hotter, *faster* and *faster* and *hotter* and *harder* and *harder* until OHHHH GOD-DDDDDDD they suddenly find that they have a bad case of sticky keyboard, if you get my drift.

Q. *That's disgusting!*
A. Yes.

Q. *Could you give an example?*
A. Certainly:

Born2Bone: I want you NOW
HunniBunni: I want YOU now
Born2Bone: I want to take off your clothes
HunniBunni: Yes! YES!
Born2Bone: I'm taking off your clothes
HunniBunni: OH YESSSS

(LONGISH PAUSE)

HunniBunni: Is something wrong?
Born2Bone: I can't unhook your brassiere
HunniBunni: I'll do it
Born2Bone: Thanks. Oh my god! I'm touching your, umm, your . . .
HunniBunni: Copious bosoms?
Born2Bone: Yes! Your copious bosoms! I'm touching them!
HunniBunni: YES!
Born2Bone: Both of them!

HunniBunni: YESSS!!

Born2Bone: I'm taking off your panties!

HunniBunni: You already did.

Born2Bone: Oh, OK. You're naked! I'm touching your entire nakedness!

HunniBunni: YESSSSSS!!!

Wazootyman: Anybody here from Texas?

Born2Bone: No

HunniBunni: No

Born2Bone: I am becoming turgid in my manfulness!

HunniBunni: YES! YES YOU ARE!! YOU ARE A BULL! YOU ARE MY GREAT BIG RAGING BULL STALLION!

Wazootyman: Hey, thanks

HunniBunni: Not *you*

Born2Bone: I AM A STALLION! I AM A RAGING, BULGING BULL STALLION, AND I AM THRUSTING MY . . . MY . . . ummm . . .

HunniBunni: Your love knockwurst?

Born2Bone: YES! I AM THRUSTING MY LOVE KNOCKWURST INTO YOUR . . . YOUR . . .

HunniBunni: Promise you won't laugh?

Born2Bone: Yes

HunniBunni: My passion persimmon

Born2Bone: Ha ha!

HunniBunni: You promised!

Born2Bone: Sorry. OK, here goes: I AM THRUST-ING MY MASSIVE KNOCKWURST OF LOVE INTO YOUR PASSION PERSIMMON!

HunniBunni: YES! YES! YES!

Born2Bone: OHHH! IT FEELS SO GOOD!! I FEEL POWERFUL!!

HunniBunni: YOU *ARE* POWERFUL, BORN2-BONE!! I FEEL YOUR POWER INSIDE ME!!!

Born2Bone: IT FEELS LIKE, LIKE . . .

HunniBunni: Like what?

Born2Bone: IT FEELS JUST LIKE, OHMIGOD-OHMIGOD . . .

HunniBunni: TELL ME, BORN2BONE!! TELL WHAT IT FEELS LIKE!!

Born2Bone: OH GOD IT FEELS LIKE . . . *IT FEELS LIKE WHEN I BREAK A TIE VOTE IN THE SENATE!!!*

(PAUSE)

HunniBunni: What did you say?

Born2Bone: Whoops

HunniBunni: It feels like when you *break a tie vote in the Senate?*

Born2Bone: Umm, listen, what I meant was . . .

HunniBunni: This is *you*, isn't it, Al? *ISN'T IT??* YOU *BASTARD!!!* YOU TOLD ME YOU WERE ATTENDING A STATE FUNERAL THIS AFTERNOON!!!

Born2Bone: *Tipper?*

HunniBunni: Whoops

Q. *Aside from chatting, what else can I do on the Internet?*
A. You can join one of the thousands of forums

wherein people, by posting messages, discuss and debate important scientific, historical, philosophical, and political topics of the day.

Q. *Like what?*
A. Barry Manilow.

Q. *There's a forum for* Barry Manilow?
A. There's a forum for *everything*.

Q. *What happens on these forums?*
A. Well, on the Barry Manilow forum, for example, fans post messages about how much they love Barry Manilow, and other fans respond by posting messages about how much *they* love Barry Manilow, too. And then sometimes the forum is invaded by people posting messages about how much they *hate* Barry Manilow, which in turn leads to angry countermessages and vicious name-calling that can go on for *months*.

Q. *Just like junior high school!*
A. But even more pointless.

Q. *Are there forums about sex?*
A. Zillions of them.

Q. *What do people talk about on those?*
A. Barry Manilow.

Q. *No, really.*
A. OK, they talk about sex, but it is *not* all titillating.

Often you'll find highly scientific discussions that expand the frontiers of human understanding.

Q. *Can you give a specific example that you are not making up?*

A. Yes. Strictly for the purpose of researching this book, I checked into one of the sex forums, pretty much at random, and I found a series of related messages, or "thread," on the topic of "How to do the BUZZ!" It turns out that the Buzz is a sexual technique.[3] In the opening message of this thread, an enthusiastic advocate—who apparently is a doctor—explains, in semi-clinical detail, how to perform this technique. Here's an excerpt:

> You pucker up your lips to form an O, then buzzzzzzzzz so that your lips are vibrating. You can practice on your finger. When your lips are vibrating on your finger, that's the sensation you are aiming at. It is rather like playing a trumpet when you don't blow but PHEbbbbbbbbbbbbbt.

This message ends with the following warning:

> Women, if you are buzzing a man . . . NEVER, NEVER, buzz the hole at the top (urethra). Likewise for men doing a woman, NEVER, NEVER, blow or buzz directly into the vaginal opening. It is possible to force air into the circulatory system so that an air bubble will form and can cause a stroke, and brain

3. Duh.

damage or heart failure. So, suck is OK, but BLOW is not!

Are you starting to see the benefits of the Information Superhighway? Already we have learned an exciting new sexual technique that, if we do it wrong, could kill our partner!

But that's just the beginning of this thread. The next message, apparently from another doctor, strongly disputes the contention that the Buzz poses medical dangers, calling it "unbelievable" and "pseudo-medical hokum."

This statement is in turn disputed by the *next* message, which states, authoritatively, that the original warning is correct, and that "it's documented in any decent medical textbook."

(Think of it: The Buzz is *documented in medical textbooks.*)

This is followed by more authoritative-sounding posts, also apparently from members of the medical profession, concerning the dangers involved in blowing air into people's orifices. Here's another excerpt:

> When I was in practice there had been a number of cases reported in the literature of people forcing air into both the rectum and urethra with very damaging, and in some cases fatal results. . . . This was usually compressed air from a compressor, or noncompressed air from a vacuum cleaner.

At this point the discussion, as is often the case on Internet forums, branches off in a new direction:

While we are on a medical topic here is something I've been wondering about: I visit a "hands on" lap-dancing club in San Francisco, and would like to know if there is any medical danger from licking breasts. I'm serious about this—undoubtedly the 22-year-olds I lick have just come from some other guy that's been licking her too. Does spit evaporate or something? Or does it stay on for the next guy to lick up??

The thread ended at this point, but I have no doubt that eventually there were more messages from concerned individuals from all over the world wishing to advance the frontiers of human understanding on the vital topic of diseases transmitted via breast spit.

Q. *It is a beautiful thing, the Internet.*
A. It is.

Q. *What is the "World Wide Web"?*
A. The World Wide Web is the multimedia version of the Internet, where you can get not only text but also pictures and sounds on a semi-infinite range of topics. This information is stored on "Web pages," which are maintained by companies, institutions, and individuals. Using special software, you can navigate to these pages and read, look at, or listen to all kinds of cool stuff. It would not surprise me to learn that, by the time you read these words, somewhere on the Web you can look at an actual electron microscope image of a molecule of breast spit.

Q. *Wow! How can I get on the Web?*

A. It's easy! Suppose you're interested in buying a boat from an Australian company that has a Web page featuring pictures and specifications of its various models. All you have to do is fire up your World Wide Web software and type in the company's Web page address, which will probably be an intuitive, easy-to-remember string of characters like this:

http//:www.fweemer-twirple~.com/heppledork/sockitomesockitome@fee.fie/fo/fum.

Q. *What if I type one single character wrong?*

A. You will launch U.S. nuclear missiles against Norway.

Q. *Ah.*

A. But assuming you type in the correct address, you merely press Enter, and there you are!

Q. *Where?*

A. Sitting in front of your computer waiting for something to happen. It could take weeks. Entire new continents can emerge from the ocean in the time it takes for a Web page to show up on your screen. Contrary to what you may have heard, the Internet does not operate at the speed of light; it operates at the speed of the Department of Motor Vehicles. It might be quicker for you to just go over to Australia and look at the boats in person.

Q. *Does that mean that the World Wide Web is useless?*
A. Heck no! If you're willing to be patient, you'll find that you can utilize the vast resources of the Web to waste time in ways that you never before dreamed possible.

Q. *For example?*
A. For example, recently I was messing around with a "Web browser," which is a kind of software that lets you search all of cyberspace—millions of documents—for references to a specific word or group of words. You can find pretty much everything that anybody has ever written on the Internet about that topic; it's an incredibly powerful research tool. So I decided to do a search on an issue that concerns—or should concern—all of humanity.

Q. *Tapeworms?*
A. Exactly. I entered the word "tapeworm," and the browser came up with a list of hundreds of places on the Web where that word appeared. I started checking them out at random,[4] and eventually I came to a forum in Austin, Texas, devoted to sushi.

Q. *Hey, why not?*
A. Exactly. And in this forum, I found a message, posted by sushi chef Yasuhiro Muramatsu, entitled "A Note About Salmon." Reading it, I was struck by how . . .

4. This took a lot of time; but, as a writer, I *have* a lot of time.

poetic it sounded. It was like a new, expanded kind of haiku. If you don't mind, I'd like to reproduce it here.

Q. *By all means.*
A. Thank you. Here it is:

A Note About Salmon
Yasuhiro Muramatsu

I am a sushi chef.
I have seen several worms and eggs in salmon
    fillet.
It is very rare case, but some time salmon has egg
    of "tapeworm."
It cause serious health problem, if you have it.

We don't eat raw salmon in Japan.
Only one exception is "RUIBE."
It is pre-frozen salmon (must be lower −20c, and
    more than 12hr).
So, you had better ask your sushi chef it before you
    order their raw salmon.

Salmon is one of the most affordable fish for sushi
    and sashimi.
And it is also looks good.
Therefore, a lot of Japanese restaurants are serving
    raw salmon.

I hope none of them does just slice and serve it.
I think you had better don't eat raw salmon except
    the restaurants which you can trust it.

By the way, I have never eat raw salmon.
I like Norway style marinade salmon "lox."

Q. *That is truly beautiful.*

A. Yes. And it's just one teensy little piece, one infinitesimally tiny fraction, of the gigantic, pulsating, mutating, multiplying mass of stuff out there on the Internet. Sooner or later, *everything* is going to be on there somewhere. You should be on there, too. Don't be afraid! Be like the bold explorer Christopher Columbus,[5] setting out into uncharted waters, fearful of what you might encounter, but also mindful of the old inspirational maritime saying: "If you don't leave the land, then you'll probably never have a chance to get scurvy and develop anemia, spongy gums, and bleeding from the mucous membranes."

So come on! Join me and millions of others on this exciting CyberFrontier, with its limitless possibilities for the enhancement of knowledge and the betterment of the human race!

Wazootyman is waiting for you.

---

5. E-mail address: ChrisCol@nina,pinta&santamaria.ahoy

10.
USING INTERNET "SHORTHAND"

How You Can Be Just as Original as Everybody Else

As a new person—or "newbie"—on the Internet, you'll probably be struck by the fact that a lot of the messages contain odd-looking words and punctuation. This is a kind of "shorthand" that Internet users have developed.

Much of this shorthand takes the form of "acronyms," which are chemical substances secreted by moths wishing to have sex.

No, wait, that's "pheromones." Acronyms are groups of initials—like "r.s.v.p."[1]—that stand for some commonly used phrase. Internet people love acronyms because they make communication much more effi-

---

1. Which stands for "asap."

cient, as we can see from the following typical conversation:

Person A: What's up?
Person B: Not much. <g>
Person A: LOL. HEFY? <g>
Person B: ROTFL.
Person C: PMFJ, but IMHO, OJIOGBUOLSW-
MRTJVAIFWNTMITSIHDHGCOAC.

This may look to you like a bunch of "gobbledygook," but these people are actually having an extremely witty conversation, Internet style. To help you decode it, here's a table of common Internet acronyms:

ACRONYM	MEANING
<g>	**"Grin"**

The <g> is widely used on the Internet to indicate that the writer meant the preceding statement to be humorous. Interestingly, the preceding statement is almost never even remotely humorous. Internet people apparently believe they can *make* their statements humorous by putting "<g>"'s after them.

EXAMPLES OF TYPICAL USAGE
I live in Akron. <g>
The French poet Jean Baptiste Racine was born in 1639. <g>

LOL   **"Laughing Out Loud"**
This indicates that the writer is laughing out loud. It is generally used in response to a statement that has a "<g>" after it.

EXAMPLE
Person A: We had some rain today. <g>
Person B: LOL

ROTFL   **"Rolling On The Floor Laughing"**
This is used in response to a statement that is *even funnier* than one that is merely LOL. There is just no end to the hilarity on the Internet.

EXAMPLE
Person A: We had some rain today, but it turned to sleet. <g>
Person B: ROTFL

HEFY?   **"Hot Enough For You?"**
This hilarious "zinger" always gets everybody ROTFL.

PMFJ   **"Pardon Me For Jumping In"**
This is often used in conjunction with another acronym **IMHO,** which stands for "In My Humble Opinion." These courteous acronyms help keep the Internet civil and polite.

EXAMPLE

PMFJ, but IMHO, you suck.

OJIOGBUOLSWM RTJVAIFWNTMIT SIHDHGCOAC	"O.J. Is Obviously Guilty, But Under Our Legal System We Must Respect The Jury's Verdict, Although It Frankly Would Not Trouble Me In The Slightest If He Drove His Golf Cart Off A Cliff"

The other popular form of Internet shorthand is the emoticon. Emoticons are a very clever use of standard punctuation marks to express a human emotion. Here's how they work.

Suppose you're typing a statement such as:

I am feeling happy

The problem with this is, the reader cannot be absolutely, 100 percent *sure* what emotion you're feeling when you type this. So at the end of the sentence, you type a colon (:) followed by a closing parenthesis ( )). Now your sentence looks like this:

I am feeling happy :)

See the difference? Instead of just a flat, emotionless statement, you now have a flat, emotionless statement with a weird punctuation mark at the end. That's because, to "read" the emoticon, you have to turn this book sideways, with the right side (☞) of the page pointing down, *then* look at the emoticon. Go ahead: Turn the page sideways!

NOW TURN IT BACK, STUPID

Did you notice what happened to the punctuation marks? That's right! They formed a "smiley face" (☺)! Now your reader will know *exactly* what your emotional state was when you wrote the words: namely, a state of happiness. But that's only the beginning. By using an *opening* parenthesis after the colon instead of a *closing* one—as in ":("—you can express the *opposite* emotion from happiness—to wit, sadness. This can add real oomph to an otherwise ho-hum sentence. Consider:

Without emoticon:

> Over 7,000 men died at Gettysburg.

With emoticon:

> Over 7,000 men died at Gettysburg :(

See the difference? The readers of the second sentence, merely by turning it sideways, will immediately recognize that it is talking about a sad thing.

Of course emoticons have been around for hundreds of years, as we see from these actual reproductions from original manuscripts:

Call me Ishmael :)

Alas poor Yorick, I knew him well :(

It was the best of times :) It was the worst of times :(

But although happy and sad faces were fine for basic statements such as these, they are not adequate to convey the subtlety and nuance of Internet communications ("Anybody here from Texas?"). So over the years, Internet users have developed a vast arsenal of emoticons to express virtually every possible human emotion. Here's a partial chart, showing some of the more useful emoticons:

USEFUL INTERNET EMOTICONS

Emoticon	Meaning
:)	Happy person
:(	Sad person
:-)	Happy person with a nose
:-(	Sad person with a nose
:—(	Person who is sad because he or she has a large nose
:►(	Person who is sad because he or she has a large fish for a nose
:-D	Person laughing
:-D*	Person laughing so hard that he or she does not notice that a 5-legged spider is hanging from his or her lip
:-|	Person unsure of which long-distance company to choose
>8-O-(&)	Person just realizing that he or she has a tapeworm
;-)	Person winking
.-)	Person who can still smile despite losing an eyeball
:-0WW	Person vomiting a series of Slim Jims
:-Q	Person who just had cybersex and is now enjoying a postcoital cybercigarette
>:-Q - ⋯	Person who was enjoying a postcoital cigarette until he suddenly noticed, to his alarm, that there is some kind of discharge dribbling from his cybermember
:-{8	Person who is unhappy with the results of her breast-enlargement surgery
:V:-|	Person who cannot figure out why nobody wants to talk to him or her, little suspecting that there is an alligator on his or her head
~oE]:-|	Fisherperson heading for market with a basket on his or her head containing a three-legged octopus that is giving off smell rays
>:-[-{❤	Person who is none too pleased to be giving birth to a squirrel

11.
SELECTED WEB SITES[1]

At Last: Proof That Civilization Is Doomed

A common criticism of the Internet is that it is dominated by the crude, the uninformed, the immature, the smug, the untalented, the repetitious, the pathetic, the hostile, the deluded, the self-righteous, and the shrill. This criticism overlooks the fact that the Internet also offers—for the savvy individual who knows where to look—the tasteless and the borderline insane.

I am thinking here mainly of the World Wide Web. Whereas much of the Internet relies strictly on text, the Web is multimedia; this means that if, for example, you're setting up a Web site devoted to exploring the

1. I want to thank the good (weird, but good) people on the alt.fan group who suggested many of these sites.

near-universal human fear that a *Star Wars* character wants to consume your gonads, you can present this issue in both words *and* pictures (I'll have more on this issue later in this chapter[2]). You can also greatly advance the frontiers of scientific knowledge regarding Spam.

In researching this chapter, I spent many, many hours exploring the World Wide Web. My time was divided as follows:

Activity	Time Spent
Typing insanely complex Web addresses	2%
Waiting for what seemed like at least two academic semesters per Web page while the computer appeared to do absolutely nothing	93%
Reading snippy messages stating that there is no such Web address	2%
Retyping insanely complex Web addresses	2%
Actually looking at Web pages	1%

As you can see, it can take quite a while for a Web page to appear on your screen. The reason for the delay is that, when you type in a Web address, your computer passes it along to another computer, which in turn passes it along to another computer, and so on through as many as five computers before it finally reaches the workstation of a disgruntled U.S. Postal

2. This is a good reason to stop reading this chapter right now.

Service employee, who throws it in the trash. So when browsing the Web, you will almost certainly encounter lengthy delays, which means that it's a good idea to have something else to do while you're waiting, such as reroofing your house.

Anyway, by virtue of being diligent and not having a real job, I was eventually able to get through to quite a few Web pages, and in this chapter I'm going to describe some of the more memorable ones. But before I do, I want to stress three points:

- All the pages described here are real; I did not make any of them up, not even the virtual toilet.
- What you see here represents just a teensy-tiny fraction of the thousands upon thousands of Web pages, with new ones being created constantly. Do not assume, from what you see in this chapter, that *all* Web pages are a total waste of time; the actual figure is only about 99.999997 percent.
- By the time you read this, you may not be able to visit all of these pages. I visited most of them in mid-1996; some of them may have since gone out of existence for various reasons, such as that their creators were recalled to their home planets.

But this chapter is not intended as an exhaustive list: I just want to give you an idea of some of the stuff that's out there. So fasten your seat belt, and let's visit some of the fascinating rest stops on the Information Superhighway. We'll start, appropriately enough, with:

THE TOILETS OF MELBOURNE, AUSTRALIA

http://minyos.xx.rmit.edu.au/~s9507658/toilet/

If you're thinking about taking a trip to Melbourne, Australia, the first question you ask yourself is: "What will the toilets be like?"

The answer can be found at this Web site, which offers *detailed* reviews of selected Melbourne-area toilets. Here are some actual excerpts:

- "What a great day for a drive! Mild weather. A nice lunch. A scenic walk. First-rate toilets."
- "The other notable thing about the toilets was the toilet paper holders. They were Bowscott continuous toilet paper holders that were actually positioned up high enough."
- "On the way we stopped at Eastland shopping centre —home of the best public toilets I have seen so far. They were clean, open, and the toilet roll holders were free moving. As with the Lysterfield Lake toilets, one of the basin-style urinals was positioned lower for kids. The hand dryer was fantastic too. It was a compact, automatic Mirage dryer. Even though it was much smaller than other hand dryers, it blew out plenty of hot air."

And that is not all: From this Web site, you can jump to some of the many, *many* other toilet-related

Web sites, including a Virtual Public Restroom ("The Toilet of the Web"[3]), where you can write a virtual message and leave a virtual "poopie."[4]

GIANT COLLECTION OF VIOLA JOKES
http://www.mit.edu/people/jcb/viola-jokes.html

If you're like most people, you frequently remark to yourself: "Darn it! I have an important business presentation to make today, and I would love to 'break the ice' by opening with a viola joke, but I don't know any fresh ones!"

Well, you will never have to make that statement again, not after you visit this Web page. This is a *huge* collection of viola jokes. I suppose it's possible that somebody, somewhere, has compiled an even *bigger* collection of viola jokes, but I seriously doubt that this could be done without the aid of powerful illegal stimulants.

Much of the viola-joke humor appears to be based on the premise that that viola players are not the brightest or most talented members of the orchestra:

Q. *How can you tell when a violist is playing out of tune?*
A. The bow is moving.

Q. *What do you call a violist with two brain cells?*
A. Pregnant.

3. http://www.auburn.edu/~carltjm/restroom.html
4. Don't ask.

SELECTED WEB SITES

Some of the jokes are probably a lot more hilarious if you know something about classical music. I'm sure, for example, that many orchestra professionals slap their thighs when they hear this one:

Q. *How do you get a violist to play a passage pianissimo tremolando?*
A. Mark it "solo."

Ha ha! "Mark it 'solo'!" Whew!

Anyway, I was genuinely surprised by this Web page. I always thought of classical orchestras as somber operations where most of the musicians are very serious and hunched over to the point of bowel disorder. I had no idea that there was this level of wackiness, especially not in the string section. (The woodwinds, of course, are a different story; those dudes and dudettes are out of *control*.)

GUIDE TO CRACKERS
http://mathlab.sunysb.edu/%7Eelijah/cstuff/index.html

This is one of those ideas that you never in a million years would have had yourself, but as soon as you see it, you smack your forehead and say: "Huh?"

This page features photographs of various types of crackers—Cheez-Its, Ritz Bits, etc.—actual size. When you click on a cracker, you go to a page that gives you packaging and nutritional information. You are also encouraged to donate crackers, especially "rare and unusual crackers."

I am *sure* there is a good reason.

HUMAN TESTICLE CONSUMPTION:

Mr. T Ate My Balls
http://www.cen.uiuc.edu/~nkpatel/mr.t/index.html

Chewbacca Ate My Balls
http://www.cen.uiuc.edu/~nkpatel/chewbacca/index.html

There are some things in life that it is better to just not even think about, and one of those things is the question of what, exactly, led to the creation of these pages.

In summary, these pages present pictures of Mr. T and Chewbacca expressing—by means of comic book–style speech and thought balloons—the dramatic theme that they would like to eat your testicles.

For example, in the opening scene of the "Chewbacca Ate My Balls" page, Chewbacca is thinking, "I wish I had some BALLS to munch on . . ." In the next scene, he is thinking: "Your balls are MINE!!" And then, in a dramatic plot development reminiscent of the work of playwright Arthur Miller, Chewbacca thinks, "What? Mr. T already got yours?"

These sites also feature a Guest Book, where visitors can leave comments. The comments that I read were all very complimentary. People really respond to a universal theme like this. I myself had to lie down for a while.

THE SPAM CAM

http://www.fright.com/cgi-bin/spamcam

If you have the slightest doubt that the Internet is good for science, you should look at this page, and then you will have much more serious doubts.

This page is billed as "The page that seeks to answer the question: IS SPAM ORGANIC?" It presents close-up photographs of scientific experiments showing what happens when Spam and other types of foods are left sitting out for long periods of time. What happens is—get ready for a major scientific breakthrough—everything gets *really* disgusting.

For a while there was also a very popular Web site[5] set up by college students wishing to determine what happens to Twinkies when they are heated with torches, dropped from tall buildings, etc.,[6] but when I tried to check it out, it had been closed down by lawyers. Perhaps by the time you read this book, it will be back in operation again. Or perhaps the entire Internet will have been closed down by lawyers. Or perhaps college students will have started dropping lawyers from tall buildings. You never know with the future.

---

5. http://www.owlnet.rice.edu/~gouge/twinkies.html
6. It turns out that pretty much nothing happens.

156

PIERCING MILDRED

http://streams.com/pierce/

Who says there is no culture on the Internet? You will, after you visit this site. This is a game where you get to select a character—either Mildred or Maurice—and then you pierce that person's body parts, or decorate her or him with designer scars. Mildred and Maurice also sometimes get infected, so sometimes you have to purchase antibiotic ointment.

You may think this sounds like a fairly perverted game, but ask yourself: Is it *really* that different from Mr. and Mrs. Potato Head?

BANANA LABELS OF THE WORLD

http://www.staff.or.jp/whoiswho/ilkka/bananadir/banana labels.html

If you thought that there were basically only a couple of types of banana labels, then a visit to this site will quickly convince you that you are a stupid idiot. This site presents pictures of hundreds of banana labels, including labels commemorating historic events such as the 50th anniversary of Miss Chiquita, not to mention a label from a Big Frieda's Burro Banana. This site will also direct you to *other* banana-label pages.[7] And

7. Of *course* there are other banana-label pages.

SELECTED WEB SITES

you are invited to send in banana labels, including "virtual banana labels," which I assume means labels for virtual bananas. (My feeling about this is: fine, but they'd better not come out with virtual beer.)

WAVE TO THE CATS

http://hogwild.hamjudo.com/cgi-bin/wave

This is the perfect Web site[8] to show to the skeptic who thinks you can't do anything useful or practical on the Internet. At this site, you can click on a button that activates a motor at a remote location; the motor is attached to a large fiberboard hand, which waves back and forth at some cats, if the cats happen to be in the room at the time. You can't actually *see* this; you just get the warm feeling of satisfaction that comes from knowing that you are causing a remote, simulated hand to wave at remote, possibly nonexistent cats. You also get a nice "Thank you for your wave" message from the Web page author, as well as his description of the way the cats usually react to the hand ("Master will stare at it when it moves; the other three cats, Callie, Mutant, and Katrina, just ignore it").

I know what you're thinking, but to my knowledge, there currently is no "Spay the Cats" Web site.

---

8. This is one of many cool sites I found out about through the highly recommended Center for the Easily Amused, located at http://www.amused.com/

TROJAN ROOM COFFEE MACHINE
http://www.cl.cam.ac.uk/coffee/coffee.html

If you go to this page, you can, merely by clicking your mouse, see, from anywhere in the world, an up-to-the-second video image of the coffee machine in the Trojan Room of the University of Cambridge Computer Laboratory in England. It would be virtually impossible to calculate the time that has been saved by disseminating this information via the Web, as opposed to previous methods.

CAPTAIN AND TENNILLE APPEARANCES
http://www.vcnet.com/moonlight/CTAPPEARANCES

This page lists upcoming personal appearances by the Captain and Tennille. Using this information, you can find out exactly where this veteran duo will be making their own special brand of musical magic so that you can arrange to be on the diametrically opposite side of the Earth when they perform "Muskrat Love."

CURSING IN SWEDISH
http://www.bart.nl/~sante/enginvek.html

This is the most thorough on-line course in Swedish cursing that I am aware of. It is scholarly,

SELECTED WEB SITES

well-organized, and professional-looking; and if your computer has sound, you can click on individual phrases, and your computer will curse at you in Swedish.

Here are some of the practical Swedish curses you can learn on this Web site (I swear I am not making these up):

Han var en jävel på att fiska.
He was bloody good at fishing.

Satan! Ungen pissade på sig!
Hell! The kid wet his trousers!

Pubkillarna var ena jävlar på att pissa.
The guys at the pub were masterly at pissing.

Jag tappade den jävla tvålen
I dropped the f**king soap.

Det vore himla roligt om du kom till festen.
It would be heavenly if you could take part in the party.

Kukjävel!
F**king f**ker!

Festen kommer att gå åt skogen! 61
The party will be a real flop!

And of course the one curse you *constantly* find yourself needing to express whenever you're in Sweden . . .

När jag blir av med gipset skall du få se på sjutton!
Just wait until I have gotten rid of the plaster!

DUTCH TRAFFIC SIGNS[9]
http://www.eeb.ele.tue.nl:80/traffic/warning-e.html

Without this site, I would never have known that the Dutch have a traffic sign that means "squalls."

FEDERAL CORPSE SLICE PHOTOS
http://www.nlm.nih.gov/research/visible/photos.html

On this site you can see images taken from the government's Visible Human Project, in which two actual deceased humans, one male and one female, were frozen in gelatin and sliced into very thin slices for the benefit of science. I know what you're wondering:

SELECTED
WEB SITES

9. I found this site, along with many other excellent ones, at a *very* useful site called Useless Pages, http://www.chaco.com/useless/index.html. Check it out.

You're wondering where the government got the corpses. You will be relieved to learn that the answer is: *not* from the Internal Revenue Service Division of Taxpayer Compliance.

Or so they claim.

PEOPLE WITH TOASTERS

http://www.berksys.com/www/promotions/uNurtoaster.html

This page features photographs of people with their toasters.

FABIO

http://redwood.northcoast.com/~shojo/Fabio/fabio.html

This page features photographs of the romantic super-star mega-hunk Fabio with his toaster.

No, seriously, the photographs depict the romantic superstar mega-hunk posing in a manner that reveals his deeply passionate sensitive innermost feelings about what a studmuffin he is. What makes this site great is that you can click on the photographs, and, if your computer has sound, Fabio will say things to you, such as "Your caress is my command." Apparently he doesn't realize that you're caressing him with a mouse pointer.

DEFORMED FROG PICTURES
http://www.mncs.k12.mn.us/frog/picts.html

One summer day in 1995 some students at the Minnesota New Country School were on a Nature Studies hike. They started catching frogs, and after a bit they noticed that many of the frogs did not appear to meet standard frog specifications in terms of total number of legs, eyes, etc. So the students started a Frog Project to study this phenomenon. If you visit this Web page, you can read about their work and see actual photographs of the frogs; this will help you to become more aware of the environment, pollution, and other important topics, unless you're the kind of sicko who just wants to look at deformed frogs.

MUSICAL SAND
http://www.yo.rim.or.jp/~smiwa/index.html

If you are interested in information on musical sand (and who is not?), this is really the only place to go. This Web site offers information in both Japanese and a language that is somewhat reminiscent of English. The introduction states:

> All information concerning Musical Sand in the world ("singing sand" on beach and "booming sand"

in desert) will concentrate in this home pages. Singing properties of the sand is very sensitive to pollution, and that may be play a sensor for it.

To my regret, musical sand is on the brink of a critical position to be exterminated. If cleaning air and sea however, musical sand plays wonderful sound with action of wind and wave for us. I make show you World of Musical Sand that Mother Nature polished by spending eternal time.

Think of it: Endangered sand!

If your computer has sound capability, you can actually listen to some singing sand. It is not easy, on the printed page, to describe the eerie, almost unearthly beauty of the sound that the sand makes; the best words I can come up with are "like a vacuum cleaner trying to suck up a dead cow." I for one would hate to see Earth lose a resource like this, and I hereby urge Sting and Willie Nelson to hold some kind of benefit concert.

EXPLODING WHALE
http://www.xmission.com:80/~grue/whale

On this site you can see pictures of the now-famous incident[10] in which the Oregon State Highway Division, attempting to dispose of a large and aromatic

---

10. About ten years ago, I saw a videotape of this incident, made by a local TV station. I wrote a column about it, and somebody unfamiliar with the copyright laws put that column on the Internet. The

dead whale that had washed up on the beach, decided to—why not?—blow it up with half a ton of dynamite.

The theory was that the whale would be converted from one large unit into many small Whale McNuggets, which would then be eaten by seagulls. Unfortunately, this is not what happened. What happened was, following a massive blast,[11] large chunks of rotting whale blubber, some of them large enough to dent a car roof, rained down upon spectators several hundred yards away, and there was *still* an extremely large chunk of dead whale lying on the beach. This was not Seagull Chow. A seagull capable of eating this chunk would have to be the size of the Lincoln Memorial.

The moral here is, if another dead whale washes up on the beach in Oregon, the authorities should probably not turn the disposal job over to the State Highway Division. But if they do, I hope they sell tickets.

WORLD RECORD BARBECUE IGNITION
http://ghg.ecn.purdue.edu/oldindex.html

If this Web page doesn't make you proud to be an American, then I frankly don't know what will. This site presents the ultimate result of the effort by mem-

---

result is that for years now, people have been sending me my own column, often with notes saying, "You should write a column about this!"

11. Talk about booming sands.

bers of the Purdue University engineering department to see how fast they could get the barbecue charcoal ignited at their annual picnic. They started by blowing the charcoal with a hair dryer; then, in subsequent years, they escalated to using a propane torch, an acetylene torch, and then compressed pure oxygen.

At this point, they were lighting the charcoal very fast, but for these guys, "very fast" was not good enough. These guys had a dream, and that dream was to ignite their charcoal faster than anybody had ever done before. And thus they hit upon the idea of using liquid oxygen, the kind used in rocket engines. On this Web page you can see photos and video of an engineer named George Goble using long wooden handles to dump a bucket of liquid oxygen onto a grill containing 60 pounds of charcoal; this is followed by a fireball that, according to Goble, reached 10,000 degrees Fahrenheit. The charcoal was ready for cooking in *three seconds*.

Next time Oregon has a whale problem, maybe it should call *these* guys.

FLAMING POP-TART EXPERIMENT
http://www-personal.umich.edu/~gmbrown/tart/

It is a well-known scientific fact[12] that if you put a Kellogg's brand strawberry Pop-Tart into a toaster and

12. This has been verified on the David Letterman show.

hold the toaster lever down so that it can't pop up, after about five minutes, the Pop-Tart will turn into the Blowtorch Snack Pastry from Hell, shooting dramatic blue flames as much as a foot out of the toaster slots.

If you visit this Web page, you can see actual photos of an experiment demonstrating this spectacular phenomenon. I urge you, however, *not* to attempt to duplicate this experiment unless you are a trained science professional using somebody else's toaster, because we are talking about a powerful force with the potential for great destruction. We can only be grateful that the Nazis never learned how to harness it, although historians strongly suspect that they were working on it near the end.

Let me repeat that the Web sites described in this chapter represent just a tiny fraction of what's out there. What you really need to do is get on the Web[13] and start poking around for yourself. You'll quickly discover that what you've read about here exemplifies some of the *saner* thinking going on. So go ahead! Get on the Web! In my opinion, it's WAY more fun than television, and what harm can it do?

OK, it can kill brain cells by the billions. But you don't *need* brain cells. You have a computer.

---

13. Don't ask *me* how. I'm not an expert on computers; I only write books about them.

12.
MsPtato and RayAdverb

A Story of Love On-line

So you've been married for 17 years and 8 months to a dependable guy, Max, a *very* dependable guy, with a good job. You have three basically good kids, with the oldest, Ryan, getting to the point where he insists on wearing unattractive clothing, but thank God still a long way from tattoos.

You have a nonchallenging (OK, boring) job, but you're glad to *have* a job after 11 years at home getting most of your mental stimulation from Oprah, although you have trouble not dwelling on the fact that your boss, who makes maybe four times your salary, has maybe half your IQ, and writes "it's" when he means "its," and is the *younger* brother of somebody you used to babysit for.

You have finally, after decades of searching, found,

and would follow to another continent if she ever moved, a hairstylist who understands exactly what you mean by "just a *little* shorter."

You have a four-bedroom, four-bathroom house, which, yes, could use new carpeting, especially in the hallway where the dog threw up after it ate the entire contents of Ashley's Easter basket, but you finally got a new kitchen four years ago and you really can't complain.

In other words, you are cruising comfortably on the interstate of life, protected by the seat belt of certainty, the driver's-side air bag of routine.

You have also been blessed with one of life's greatest gifts, a real, true-blue friend, Leslie; the kind of friend who will tell you without hesitation if a suit that you sincerely lust for makes your butt look too big; the kind of friend who once, when the snotty maître d' refused to seat you because you were wearing culottes—*nice* culottes—and the restaurant had a no-shorts policy, said, loud enough to turn every head in the main dining room, "IF SHE CAN'T WEAR CULOTTES, HOW COME YOU CAN WEAR A HAIRPIECE THAT LOOKS LIKE A DEAD BEAVER??" and the two of you laughed so hard in the parking lot that you peed your culottes; the kind of friend who, when you're crying, understands *why* you're crying, and will cry with you, even though *you* may not necessarily be 100 percent sure why you're crying.

Sometimes, at the Mexican restaurant after work, after the second margarita, you tell Leslie that although your husband is—it bears repeating—dependable, he is not exactly Antonio Banderas in the romance department, or even Antonio Banderas's tax accountant. No, these days Max is more like the man who comes around every month and sprays the kitchen cabinets to forestall cockroaches—reliable, agreeable, competent, *dutiful.* You can remember—this was a time before Ashley, before Tyler, even before Ryan (God, *was* there a time before Ryan?)—when he could be, OK, not exactly *passionate,* but definitely *excitable.* Like the time at the Wasserman wedding reception, at some country club, when—champagne will do this—he talked you into making love *on the golf course,* during *daylight,* the two of you naked as jaybirds behind a tiny hill, grass sticking to your thighs, golfers all around talking about bogeys, Max whispering urgently to you, "It's OK! We're in the rough here!"

And now he'd rather play golf. And the truth is, that's pretty much OK with you. You wonder if you just naturally reach a point—your parents definitely reached this point—where you categorically reject the concept of outdoor sex, with the next logical casualty being indoor sex.

And Leslie reminds you—this is the crux of her argument—that Max is *very* dependable, and she says maybe you should take one of those getaway Love Encounter weekends, just the two of you, and you try to envision it, and what you envision is the two of you getting into the hotel room and both thinking, *Might as well get this over with*, having your Love Encounter ASAP, checking it off on the activities list, so that you can go to the beach and read your book, and Max can play golf. And Leslie, who admits that she and Stu *never* did it outdoors (Stu has allergies), says this is normal at our age; we channel our energy into other stuff—kids, careers, home improvement, gum care. And you agree that yeah, maybe this is just the way it is. And when you think about the big picture, the kids and the comfort and the kitchen, and then you factor dependability into the equation, it's really not so bad.

But you're pretty sure you still have some energy left over.

When Max and the kids bring home the computer, your only interest in it is where they think they're going to put it, and the answer is, NOT the living room, which is the only room left that you'd feel comfortable entertaining in, not that you ever entertain. But your point is that if you ever *did*, you're damned if you're going to have an oversized Nintendo game squatting among the guests.

Max and the kids insist that it's not just a toy, that you can do all *kinds* of practical things on it: Balance your checkbook! Research school reports! Learn to speak Norwegian! But whenever you walk into the living room (of *course* it ends up in the living room) you do not see them speaking Norwegian. You see them staring at some computer game and shouting at each other. Sometimes Max is shouting the loudest.

"No no NO NO, RYAN!" he's shouting. "You don't want the Sidewinder! You want the *Maverick!*"

"*Dad,*" Ryan responds, calmer than his father (he is, after all, flying the Stealth Fighter) but still very intense, "we don't *have* the Maverick. I used the Maverick to blow up the patrol boat."

"*What?*" says Max, shocked, anguished, not ready to accept the fact that his own son would do such a thing. "You don't use the Maverick against a *boat!* You use the *Harpoon!*"

"What's going ON?" you ask.

"They're over Russia," explains Tyler.

"They're shooting missiles," explains Ashley.

"Well, could we land the plane and eat dinner?" you ask, sounding, you realize, like the wife/mother character in a sitcom. There should be canned laughter.

"*Mom,*" says Ryan, the pilot, meaning "no."

"We're almost to the Primary Target," says Max, a little more apologetically, but also meaning "no."

"I wanna watch," says Tyler.

"Me too," says Ashley.

"But we're not even *enemies* with Russia," you point out. "Russia has *McDonald's.*"

"THEY'RE FIRING AT YOU!" shouts Max. "Use the ECM! Use the ECM!"

"WHICH KEY??" shouts Ryan, fingers tensed over the keyboard.

"F1!" shouts Max, pawing frantically through the manual. "NO! F2! *F2F2F2!*"

You drift back to the kitchen (it *is* a nice kitchen), and dine alone (Lean Cuisine stuffed pepper, baked potato, lemon juice) with your Amy Tan book, which maybe is what you really wanted to do anyway.

"**I** hate it," you're telling Leslie several days later, at the Mexican restaurant, referring to the computer. "It's like it's the TV set from hell, where all the shows are in a mysterious language and everybody understands them except me."

Leslie nods. She has zero grasp of computers. She is locally famous for not being able to set her own clock radio.

"Max says I can keep recipes on the computer," you say. "Like I have thousands of recipes I need to keep track of. Like I'm gonna suddenly forget how to make meat loaf, and I'll be, like, 'Oh God, how much bread crumbs do I need? Better check the computer!'"

Leslie is laughing, holding her hand to her mouth, trying not to spew nacho flecks. She is a wonderful friend.

"What about the whaddyacallit, Internet?" she asks.

"What *about* the Internet?" you ask.

"I don't know," says Leslie. "Isn't it on the computer? The Internet? That's all I see anymore in the newspaper. Internet Internet Internet."

"Maybe," you say. "But I don't know what it is, and whatever it is, I bet it's basically a whole lot of people like Max."

"So if you got on the Internet," says Leslie, "maybe Max would talk to you."

"About *what?*" you ask, and you both laugh. Thank God for margaritas.

Two weeks later, you're in the family room, sorting through an enormous pile of old issues of *National Geographic*, wondering if anybody in the history of the world has ever actually *read* an old issue of *National Geographic*. The only other person at home is Ashley, who is (naturally) on the computer, using America OnLine, which you are none too crazy about because the bill last month was $43.08. She's been quiet for about 15 minutes, when suddenly . . .

"MOM!" she calls. "WHAT'S A BLOWJOB?"

Hurling aside the September 1982 issue of *National Geographic* ("Tree Snails of the Amazon"), you stride very briskly into the dining room and, in the calmest voice you can manage, ask, "What did you say, honey?"

"What's a blowjob?"

"Where did you hear that word, honey?"

"From SnakeNose."

"Who is that, honey?"

"Somebody in the chat room."

"What is that, honey?"

"*Mom*," says Ashley, unwilling to squander another second of her busy life trying to explain things to grown-ups, "WILL YOU PLEASE JUST TELL ME WHAT A BLOWJOB IS?"

That night you have a major family battle, with you on one side and the family on the other. Your position is, get rid of whatever it is putting those words on the screen, or you are going to cut off the plug with pruning shears. Their position—expressed by the kids, but with Max clearly on their side—is, c'mon, be *reasonable*, it's not really *like* that, there's a lot of *good* stuff on there, they have cool games, you can send e-mail, you can download, c'mon, Mom, *please*, you can use the Parental Controls to keep Ashley out of the grown-up chat rooms, c'mon please please *please* Mom PLEASE, until finally they succeed (Where do they *learn* this skill? Is it taught in the schools?) in making you feel like the Wicked Witch of the West, holding Toto captive in your bicycle basket, and you say OK, they can keep America OnLine, but if this happens ONE MORE TIME blah blah blah, but of course they're no longer really listening to you, because they know the battle is over and they won.

That night, in bed, when Max gives you the peck on the cheek that 97 percent of the time passes for your sex life, you tell him that if Ashley turns into a slut and gets pregnant at age 13, he had better never, ever, fall asleep in your house again, because you're not going to make the same mistake Lorena Bobbitt made, the mistake of throwing it where the police could find it.

The following evening, determined not to be the last person on Earth to know what the hell is going on, you start attempting to learn how to work the computer. You get your first lesson from Tyler and Ashley, who show great patience and understanding for a full 45 seconds, after which they start rolling their eyes and grabbing the mouse out of your hands, scooting the little pointer arrow around the screen, making things suddenly appear and disappear. You are totally lost. They can't *believe* how dense you are.

"*Mom,*" says Ashley (you remember when she regularly put her shorts on backward), "you have to *double-click* it."

"But how are you supposed to *know* that?" you ask, and their eyes almost roll out of their heads, because *everybody* knows that. Ashley and Tyler were *born* knowing that.

But you don't know anything. You don't know what "dragging" is; or why sometimes you have to press the *left* mouse button and sometimes you have to press the *right* one; or where things go when they disappear from the screen; or how to make them come back; or why the computer sometimes emits a disapproving "ding." You are a Paleolithic woman trying to land a 747, assisted only by idiot-savant munchkins with microscopic attention spans. At the end of your "lesson," you

MSPTATO AND RAYADVERB

have concluded that basically what you can do with a computer is move a bunch of boxes around the screen, and you're thinking: That's *it*? That's *Cyberspace*?

It is Ryan—getting older, slowly but surely morphing into a human—who finally takes the time to show you how to use the computer to actually *do* something, namely write. The first time you produce a document (a letter to your mother), and you see it come out of the printer crisp and perfect, with exactly the font you picked (you went with "Arial" after deciding that "Braggadocio" was a little too much for Mom), you think: Hey, *cool*.

"It's, I don't know, it's kind of fun," you're telling Leslie.

"Fun?" Leslie asks. "Writing a letter to your mother is *fun*?"

"Well," you say, not believing this is you, saying this, "there's other stuff you can do."

"Like what?"

"Like, OK, you can keep your calendar on there."

"YES!" says Leslie. "Your calendar! Of course! So you can keep track of all the appointments in your busy life! Just like Martha Stewart!"

She has you laughing.

"*May 2nd, 7:15* A.M.," she says, in an important, businesslike voice. "*Purchase bagel on way to work. Toasted! With cream cheese! No chives!*"

"June 4th, 10:30 P.M.," you say. "Ask Max for maybe the 623rd time to please put his dirty, funky underwear in the damn hamper and not leave it sitting ON THE BUREAU for four days like some kind of damn art object!"

Leslie is hooting, putting her hand on yours to let you know she knows this conversation applies to both of you.

"I got it!" she says. "Your calendar could *interface with your recipes!*"

"YES!" you shout, startling the waiter. "*August 23rd, 5:30 P.M., preheat oven to 375 degrees!*"

"*5:37 P.M., MINCE TWO CLOVES GARLIC!*" shrieks Leslie, and you both collapse facedown on the table, gals in a giggle storm, laughing at your calendars, at your lives.

You really do kind of like the computer, though.

It is, once again, Ryan who shows you how to get on to America OnLine. He explains that you need to pick a screen name, which is the name you use when you're signed on. Some people use their real names, but most use an alias. That's what you decide to do. You'll have a Secret Identity, like Wonder Woman.

"Nobody knows who you really are on there," Ryan says. "Some people, you don't know if they're men or women or what, or how old or anything. Like, sometimes they think I'm like this twenty-five-year-old man."

"Who thinks that?" you ask.

"Never mind," he says.

It takes you a while to select a screen name, because a lot of the ones you want—"WonderWomn," for example—are already taken. You wind up trying variations of your childhood nickname, "Tater," and finally settle for "MsPtato." Feeling a little silly, you type this in, then type in your password, which is your maiden name, and then there you are . . . on the Internet! Which looks like more screen boxes.

"What do I do?" you ask Ryan.

"Click on the chat area," he says, pointing to a little icon of a woman whispering into a man's ear. You click on it, and a new box appears on your screen, with the words:

OnlineHost: *** You are in "Lobby 67". ***

Immediately words start appearing on the screen and scrolling upward. You realize it's a conversation, but a disjointed, time-delayed, mutant conversation, with everybody responding to something somebody else said several statements earlier, on top of which nobody really seems to have anything in common—they, like you, were just tossed in here by the America OnLine computer, forming the World's Most Random Discussion Group.

You watch the words (at least some of them are words) zip past:

Ejsprit90202: hello
Proooooof: wuz up all ??

Tryptchon: looking for fem to fem cyber

Proooooof: ej you m/f?

Bpwedg8876: Micigan . . . how do you like living there SW?

Ejsprit90202: f/19 - u?

CHURPLAF: ANY FEMALS

SwtstONE45: it's cool thanx for asking bp !

Proooooof: 30/m

Jason968738: POOP

Jason968738: POOP

Jason968738: POOP

Jason968738: P

Jason968738: O

CHURPLAF: EJ LETS GO PRIVAT

"That means go to a private room, just you and the other person," says Ryan.

You nod, watching the screen.

Lv74lace12: define fem to fem

Jason968738: O

Jason968738: P

Bpwedg8876: I always wanted to visit up North . . . in Ga. now.

Proooooof: jas your an ashole

SwtstONE45: my aunt lives in ga. macon !

Tryptchon: woman to woman

"Go ahead," says Ryan. "Type something."

"Type *what?*" you ask. "I don't know what anybody's talking about."

"It doesn't matter," says Ryan. "Just type hello."

You type "Hello." And there it is, your first public screen appearance:

MsPtato: Hello.
Jason968738: PROOF EAT SHIT
SwtstONE45: i lived in sweden 3 years and it was snow snow snow
CHURPLAF: LETS GET IT ON LADES
Proooooof: mspot m/f?

"Answer him," says Ryan.

"Answer who?" you ask.

"The Proof guy," says Ryan, pointing at the screen. "He's asking if you're 'm' or 'f.' You type 'f.'"

"I *know* I'm an 'f,'" you say, typing "f" and seeing:

Lv74lace12: doing what, trp?
MsPtato: f
Jason968738: PROF YOU SUCK
Bpwedg8876: I heard swede was a beatiful place
TheDwornSter: hey room
Tryptchon: want 2 find out lv?
CHURPLAF: MSPOTO LETS GET IT ON

"Um," says Ryan, grabbing the mouse and quickly clicking you out of Lobby 67, "there's a lot of other stuff on here."

"I bet there is," you say.

And there is. Over the next few nights, you click your way into all *kinds* of places, including Married and Flirting, Bored Housewives (which turns out to be mostly males hoping to talk dirty to, or pretending to be, bored housewives), Over 40, Physicians Online, M4M (this means "men for men," a fact that you discover when you are asked explicitly about your penis length), Car Problems, Nude at the Computer, UFOs, Witches, and Deranged Maniacs, to name only a few. You are shocked, repelled, fascinated. You are also hit on many, many times, usually crudely and immediately, although sometimes they ask you where you're from first (this is the on-line version of foreplay). You understand that the attention is not flattering; that there is a vast, relentless, indiscriminate tide of male horniness surging through the chat areas.

"I don't know why it's called 'chat,'" you're telling Leslie, making air quotation marks around the word "chat" with your fingers. "I mean, it's like saying a bull is 'chatting' when he's grunting on top of a cow. These guys are *horny*, and they're *everywhere*."

"Sign me up!" says Leslie.

"I don't know," you say. "A lot of them are gross and illiterate. Like they say, 'Your so funny,' with no apostrophe in 'you're.' That really turns me off, you know?

It's like when you're talking to somebody, and you suddenly notice he has a major case of neck hair."

"So you *do* chat with them," says Leslie.

"Well, some of them, until they get gross or boring," you say, "or until I figure out they're Ryan's age, which a whole lot of them are."

"*Hmm,*" says Leslie, pretending to think about it, "Ryan's kinda cute."

"Leslie!"

"So really, if they're such losers, why do you keep doing it?"

"I don't know," you say, "it's kind of fun, the game of it, not knowing who's out there. And it's nice, just for a while, to not feel like such a *mom.*"

"**M**OM," says Tyler, one inch from your ear to make sure you can hear. "PLEASE. We wanna play Wing Commander."

"In a minute," you say, clicking furiously at the keyboard.

"MOM YOU BEEN ON THERE ABOUT 900 GAZILLION HOURS," points out Ashley, who is not exaggerating all that much, judging from the last America OnLine bill, for $143.62. (Thank God you balance the checkbook.)

"I'm almost done, now *stop asking me or you will not be allowed to use the computer,*" you say, as if you have important work to finish here; they mope out of the room, dragging their feet, Abused Children.

You have friends now on-line. Mostly women, but also some men—cronies, mostly older guys, not sex fiends (although there is much harmless crony-style innuendo-laden banter). You know how to locate them when you sign on; you know how to send them Instant Messages that pop up on their screens; you know how to set up chat areas for just your group; you know what's going on in their lives (not much, they all complain, but the complaining is amusing and reassuring).

You also know how to get on the *real* Internet, the huge, wild one outside the walls of the America OnLine cyber-themepark; you know how to read and post messages on newsgroups; you find that you're sometimes ridiculed because your e-mail address identifies you as an AOLer, which is considered by status-conscious Net denizens to be totally uncool, the lowest of the low.

"Can you BELIEVE those pretentious assholes?" you message your cronies, in the chat area where you hang out. "Feeling superior because of their INTERNET ADDRESS? Are they geeks or WHAT??"

That comment gets you "LOL" (meaning, you have learned, "Laughing Out Loud") responses from the cronies, but when you tell Leslie about it, she looks at you blankly and says, "What, there's different parts of the Internet?"

You're not seeing Leslie as much as you used to. More and more, when she calls to see if you're up for the Mexican restaurant, you say, "Oh, gee, thanks, but I can't."

What you don't say is: *Because I want to get on the computer.*

It's 1:30 A.M. on a Tuesday, and the kids are asleep, and so is Max, who stomped to the bedroom after you and he had one of those toweringly stupid fights that only seriously married people can have, the original cause being—you can hardly believe this—who should call the man who was supposed to have fixed the garage-door opener but did not. This quickly escalated into an all-embracing, multi-tentacled, giant squid of a fight, the kind that puts much angry ink in the water. Fights like that, you and Max have learned, aren't resolved by talking; they're resolved by the gradual rotation of Earth, which is what you're both waiting for now—Max in the bedroom, stewing, then snoring; you, once again, on-line.

None of your cronies are signed on; it's just you and the usual collection of apostrophe-impaired sleazeballs. You're scrolling through the sad, desperate list of member-created chat rooms:

M Needs Fat Fem
Married and Looking
SOUL MATE SEARCH
Submissive Husband
Skirts and Knee Sox
SHAVERS ONLY
Hot Older Female

186

Buxom Women
Smooth M 4 Hairy M

Next to the list is a box labeled "Create Member Room." Figuring, what the hell, you click on it, and type in: "Can Actually Spell." You click on OK, and there you are:

OnlineHost: *** You are in "Can Actually Spell". ***

In the upper-right corner of the screen, there's a little box telling you who's in the room. For several minutes it's just MsPtato. You're about to quit, concluding you can't compete with SHAVERS ONLY (whatever the hell *that* means), when he appears on your screen:

RayAdverb: You can SPELL? On America OnLine? Is that ALLOWED?

Laughing, you answer.

MsPtato: Don't tell anybody!
RayAdverb: Well, I guess I can let you off, as long as you don't punctuate properly.
MsPtato: I wouldn't dream of it; really, I wouldn't.
RayAdverb: A semicolon! In Cyberspace! Be still my heart!
MsPtato: I'd show you my ellipsis, but we barely know each other . . .

Great line! Under pressure! You pump your fist, congratulating yourself.

RayAdverb: So, what's a literate, intelligent person doing here at this hour?

MsPtato: I don't know what a literate, intelligent person is doing, but I'M hanging out aimlessly while my brain cells die one at a time. And you?

RayAdverb: Same thing, definitely. It's hard for me to get on here during normal hours, with all the time my son spends playing that Federation game. AOL must LOVE that.

MsPtato: My son's on there endlessly. He tells me he's worth millions of "groats." That's the money they use there, I think.

RayAdverb: Yeah. I tell Nate, "Great! Groats! Can we use those to pay the AOL bill?"

So we both have kids. So this is totally innocent, right? *Right?*

MsPtato: "OK," she said inquiringly, "why 'RayAdverb?'"

RayAdverb: Dull answer: My name's Ray, and I'm an English teacher (high school). What about "MsPtato"?

MsPtato: Even duller: childhood nickname.

RayAdverb: They called you "Ptato"? Was there a vowel shortage? You grew up during the Grt Dprssn?

MsPtato: Don't make me laugh; it'll wake everybody up.

RayAdverb: ANOTHER semicolon! You brazen temptress! Who's "everybody"?

MsPtato: "So," she said, changing the subject, "is it interesting, being an English teacher?"

RayAdverb: It is, pardon my French, boring as shit. But I am by God going to MAKE it interesting, to keep you online.

And he does, until 4:45 A.M. It is *amazing*. It is *perfect*. It is three hours of effortlessly fascinating talk; you agree on everything, hate the same things, get each other's jokes instantly. It's the Vulcan Mind Meld, the two of you *connecting*, as though your souls are flowing through the phone line, coming together, *fusing*.

He's married with two kids, boy 10, girl 6. His wife is "nice" and a "good person." He's two years younger than you.

You agree to exchange photos (you're going to send the one of you in Kauai, wearing the green print halter top and white shorts; the one where your calves look really good). You also agree, knowing that this is not how guilt-free people act, that you'll send your picture to his school, and he'll send his to your office.

He lives six hours away.

This is scary.

The next morning, this is how Max apologizes: "I'll call the damn guy."

"No, it's OK," you say. "I'll do it. I'm sorry."

"Well," he says, "I'm sorry too."

"No, Max, I'm . . ."

Max is looking at you.

". . . I'm just really sorry. I'll call him."

You're weeping, and you don't really know why, although exhaustion is surely a factor.

"You OK?" he asks.

"Fine, I'm fine," you say. "Go ahead. You'll be late. I'll get the kids going. I'm sorry."

"I'm sorry, too," says Max, not sure why he is, but happy to be escaping the Weep Zone.

The instant you hear the garage door close (manually), you go to the computer, turn it on, start up America OnLine. It seems to take forever to log you on and then . . .

YOU HAVE MAIL, the box says.

You click it eagerly, and there it is:

Dear Goddess of Punctuation—
That was AMAZING . . .
    I'm gonna make the little bastards write an essay today, so I can just sit there, pretending to read Important Teacher Documents, while I think about you.
RayAdverb

You read it again, and again, and again. You go to the hallway, yell up the stairs: "KIDS! C'MON! YOU'RE GONNA BE LATE!"

You go back to the computer, read it again:

That was AMAZING . . .

That morning at work, you are Lost in Space. You stare for 45 minutes at a two-paragraph memorandum generated by a corporate attorney whose sole legal purpose appears to be to prove that he has no idea what "parameter" means.

This is ridiculous, you tell yourself, not meaning the memorandum. *People don't . . . You can't just . . . Not in three hours, typing to a complete . . . You don't KNOW anything about . . . Grow UP! Get REAL! You're a MOTHER! You're a WIFE! You have a FAIRLY NEW KITCHEN!*

You mail the photo at lunch.

"Mom," says Ryan at dinner (spaghetti; sauce from the Prego jar) "you look terrible."

"Why *thank* you, dear," you say, trying for a June Cleaver sound.

"I hate Josh," announces Ashley.

"Who's Josh?" asks Tyler.

"A boy in my school and he takes stuff out of his nose," says Ashley.

"*Gross*," says Tyler, chewing.

"You OK?" Max asks you.

"Yeah," you say, "I just didn't sleep well. I'm fine."

"OK," says Max, never one to probe. *But very dependable, dammit.*

"And then he wipes it on your sandwich," says Ashley.

"*EWWWW*," says Tyler, twirling up another forkful.

"Mom," says Ryan, "can I play Federation?"

"OK," you say, "but not too long." *Because I need to get on there and talk to him and see if I'm out of my mind.*

Finally, *finally*, the kids are upstairs. Max is watching TV. You're signing on as fast as your fatigued, fumbling fingers will function.

YOU HAVE MAIL, the box says. You click.

Will you be on tonight? Around 11:30? I hope? Are you going insane, too? Please say yes.

"Yes," you tell the screen.

You message your cronies. They're all still amused by how boring their lives are. "Same old same old," they type.

"Same here," you type; then you look at your watch.

"You still up?" asks Max, heading for bed with his golf magazine, which he regularly sleeps with.

"Yeah, I'm feeling better," you say, trying to sound perky. "I think I'll stay up for a while."

11:26:38
   11:26:39
   11:26:40
   11:26:41

"Ding," says the computer, and your heart—actually, your stomach—leaps as a box appears with the words "Instant Message from RayAdverb," and there he is:

RayAdverb: So I'm thinking, who needs to sleep?.
MsPtato: Sleep is definitely overrated.
RayAdverb: This is crazy, right? Isn't this crazy? Are we crazy?
MsPtato: Yes. Yes. Yes.
RayAdverb: I mean, I'm sitting here, in this same old family room, in this same old house with the same old furniture and the same old septic tank that backs up every spring, but I'm not here at ALL.
MsPtato: I know EXACTLY what you mean. I'm not here, either.
RayAdverb: So where ARE we?
MsPtato: We're in this little Instant Message box.
RayAdverb: I love it in here.

There's the word. You're staring at it. You can't think of anything to type.

RayAdverb: Well, I *do* love it.
MsPtato: Well, me too.

Four days (and maybe 10 hours of sleep) later, at the office, you find a manila envelope from him in your mail. You walk in a rapid but (you hope) businesslike way back to your cubicle, open the envelope, and pull out a note (he prints neatly) saying: "So, here's a picture of me, unless you don't like the way I look, in which case here's a picture of my much uglier brother, FredAdverb."

You shake out the picture, which lands facedown on your desk. You fumble at it, turn it over, look at his face.

He's *cute.*

Damn. What are you gonna *do?*

MsPtato: Hey, you never told me you were *cute*.
RayAdverb: Well, you never said you were sultry and had great legs.
MsPtato: You mean you actually believed that was a picture of ME?
RayAdverb: Well, my immediate reaction was that it was a young Sophia Loren, but smarter and with better typing skills.
MsPtato: Flatterer! Go on.
RayAdverb: Listen (he takes a deep breath)—I want to meet you.

Damn.

MsPtato: You mean, In Person? Outside of the Instant Message Box?

RayAdverb: Maybe it would be harmless.

MsPtato: Ho ho ho.

RayAdverb: OK, it wouldn't be harmless. But would it be harmFUL?

MsPtato: Oh, God, I'm starting to feel like Francesca in *The Bridges of Madison County.*

RayAdverb (horrified): No!

MsPtato: Yes! I'm a character in a bad book!

RayAdverb: And I am the highway and a peregrine and all the sails that ever went to sea.

MsPtato: My God! You READ it! You! An English teacher!

RayAdverb: I read it; I thought it was pathetic; I thought it was smarmy; I thought it was pretentious trash. And when Francesca found out that Robert was dead, I was depressed for a week.

Damn. You have to meet this guy.

"**S**o OK," you're saying to Leslie, two weeks later, "let's say hypothetically you're attracted to this man."

"What man?" says Leslie, instantly on Full Red Alert.

You're staring into your margarita.

"*What man?*" demands Leslie. "That guy from work? Steve? The one who shows you his forearms?"

"No!" you say. "Yuck. No, it's nobody at work. It's nobody you know, nobody around here. I mean, I haven't even *met* him."

"Ah," says Leslie. "Mel Gibson. Join the club."

"No," you say, laughing. "I mean, I haven't *met* him, but I *know* him."

"How do you . . . Wait, is this a *computer* friend?"

You look at her, a little embarrassed.

"You're attracted to one of the dirty-talking *losers?*"

"No, no, he's not one of those. He's nothing like those. He's an English teacher, and he's really nice, and funny, and . . . I mean, we talk every night. *Every night.* For *hours.*"

"Max doesn't notice this?"

"Max wouldn't notice if I grew a beard."

"What do you talk about?"

"Everything. *Everything.* The way we connect, it's almost *scary.* I can tell him *anything,* and he always just *knows.* And it's like, when I'm talking to him—OK, this is going to sound like a cliché, but—that's the only time I feel *alive.*"

"I bet he hates golf."

"Oh yes," you say, laughing.

"OK, so you like this person," she says. "But how can you be *attracted* to him if you don't even know what he looks like?"

"I do. He sent a picture."

"And?"

"And I think he's cute."

"Let me see."

"It's at work."

"Did you send him a picture?"

"Yes."

"The one with the halter top and the calves?"

"Yes."

"Good choice."

(What a *great* friend.)

"I don't know," she says. "I mean, with a picture, you can't always tell. What if he's, let's say, really tremendously short? What if he has B.O.?"

"He doesn't have B.O."

"How do you *know* that?"

"I just know."

"You know this man's bodily-aroma status from the way he *types*?"

"Yes."

Leslie looks at you, right into your eyes, a long time. Your best friend.

"Girl," she pronounces, "you are *gone*."

RayAdverb: We don't have to decide now.

MsPtato: But I *want* to decide. I'm going *crazy*. I never sleep anymore. I never think about anything but this.

RayAdverb: I know, I know. Listen, we could try the

phone, see how we sound to each other. Maybe you'll hate my voice. Maybe I'll sound like Ross Perot.

"Excuse me," says Max, in the doorway, in a tone of voice that does not mean excuse me. "Could you please tell me how my golf shoes got on the patio?"

"I'm sorry. They were muddy, so I . . ."

"I *know* they were muddy. I was going to *clean* them, OK? That's why I put them in the goddamn *kitchen*, OK?"

This is of course not really about the golf shoes; this is about your most recent argument, which was about why there was only one-sixteenth (well, *Max* says one-sixteenth; you see it as closer to an eighth) of a tank of gas left in the minivan. The argument is over, but the Earth hasn't rotated much, and the anger is still in the air.

"I'm sorry," you say. "I was just . . ."

"Just, next time, just *leave the shoes there*, OK?" says Max, walking out.

"I'm sorry," you say again. "I'm sorry."

You turn back to the keyboard.

MsPtato: I'm afraid of what will happen if we talk on the phone.
RayAdverb: Because . . .
MsPtato: Because we'll be letting this out of the Instant Message box. I'm afraid of that. Aren't you?

RayAdverb: Yes, a little. OK, a lot. But, DAMN. You know?

MsPtato: Yup. I know.

"MOMMMMM," screams Ashley, from upstairs.

"WHAT, HONEY?" you call toward the hall.

"TYLER'S SCARING ME WITH HIS TOOTH-BRUSH!"

"I AM NOT!"

"HE IS TOO. HE'S MAKING IT SAY VAMPIRE NOISES AND HE'S TURNING OFF THE LIGHT!"

"I AM NOT!"

"TYLER, STOP IT RIGHT NOW," you yell.

"SHE SAID STOP IT RIGHT NOW," yells Ashley, a squeaky-voiced echo of you.

RayAdverb: So, do we just stop?

MsPtato: Stop what? Stop thinking? Stop feeling?

RayAdverb: Stop talking about it. Maybe that'd help.

MsPtato: No.

RayAdverb: Right. No.

MsPtato: God, I HATE this.

RayAdverb: You hate this?

MsPtato: No, I love this.

RayAdverb: OK, listen: I love you. OK? There.

"MOMMMMMMM! TYLER SAYS THERE'S A BAT!"

"I DID NOT!"

"TYLER!" you yell. You should make a tape recording.
"YOU ALWAYS BELIEVE HER!"

MsPtato: Listen, I love you, too.
RayAdverb: Oh Lord, that looks good.
MsPtato: But I don't know what to do.
RayAdverb: If you scroll upward, you'll see where I said, quote, we don't have to decide now.
MsPtato: Then I will be an insane woman.
RayAdverb: Good. We can be insane lovers in an Instant Message Box.

"MOMMMMMMMMMMM!!"

MsPtato: Can we do that?
RayAdverb: We've *been* doing that. And maybe someday we'll leave the box.
MsPtato: But maybe not.
RayAdverb: I can live with maybe not.

"MOMMMMMMMMMMMMMMMMM!!!!"

MsPtato: Listen, I have to go.
RayAdverb: OK. Just come back.
MsPtato: I will. I will for sure come back to our box.
RayAdverb: I will for sure be here.
MsPtato: Bye, cutie. I'm crying.
RayAdverb: I know. Me too.

Ryan comes into the dining room as you're signing off; he looks at you.

"You OK, Mom?"

"I'm fine, honey," you say, trying for a smile. "Really."

"You done with the computer?"

"I am," you say, turning toward the stairs, toward the sound of the sibling squall.

"I'm done with the computer. For right now."

THE END

For Right Now

13.
CONCLUSION

The Future of the Computer Revolution

OR

Fun with Mister Johnson

In setting out to write this book, I wanted to make the Computer Revolution understandable to the average, nontechnical person, defined as "the person who cannot open a childproof aspirin bottle without using an ax."

I knew this task would not be easy, because (a) there are a lot of extremely complex technical issues involved, and (b) I did not plan to do any research. Nevertheless I have tried, in these pages, to provide you with information that would be of immense practical value if not for the fact that it all became obsolete minutes after I wrote it. I might as well have written this book in Swahili for all the good it's going to do you, because in the Computer Revolution everything nanges way too fast for the human brain to comprehend. This is why only 14-year-olds[1] really understand what's going on.

For example, I have referred many times in this book to the hugely popular Windows 95☺☺ operating system, but of course as soon as everybody has purchased and learned to actually *use* Windows 95⁺, it will be replaced by something newer, something better, something totally different, and something that—above all—requires you to give more money to Microsoft. The cycle of obsolescence has become so short that, in the computer superstores of tomorrow, there will be Dumpsters located conveniently right next to the cash registers so you can discard your obsolete purchases immediately after paying for them, then go back into the store and buy something even newer.

So the bottom line is, if you think the Computer Revolution is anywhere *near* over, then you are, with all due respect, a moron. The Computer Revolution is just getting cranked up. We have no idea what computers will be like ten or twenty years from now. For all we know, the Computer of the Future, rather than being a clunky external appliance, will be a miniaturized device that will be surgically implanted into your skull, where it will transmit information directly to your brain. Think of the advantages! Let's say you're a business consultant, and you're going to an important

1. No, they are *not* human.

lunch with a major potential client whom you really want to impress. Before entering the restaurant, you'd simply open your wallet, select a dime-sized micro-disk containing billions of bytes of information, and insert it into your ear. Then, during the lunch, when the potential client, testing your knowledge, asked you for some obscure data, you'd simply squeeze the bridge of your nose to activate your internal computer, and within a nanosecond you'd hear yourself, in your own natural voice, telling your potential client: "Hey, big boy! Let's play Mister Johnson Hunts for Beaver!" Because by mistake you inserted the micro-disk for Volume 27 of Hot Sex Fantasies for Men.

Yes, there is a bright new tomorrow waiting for us, and not just in the area of hardware. The Software of the Future will also be extremely sophisticated. For one thing, it will be *much* bigger and more powerful than today's software programs, which are so puny that you can fit several of them on your hard drive at the same time. The Software of the Future will have so many features, graphics, animated cartoon characters, video clips, etc., that a single program will fill up all the space on your hard drive before you're halfway through installing it. You'll need to purchase several additional computers just to get the program operating to the point where it will tell you the phone number for Technical Support.

But once you finally get the Software of the Future running, you'll be amazed at what it will do. It will be so sophisticated that it will almost seem to be a living entity. It will get to know you as a person and call you by your name. It will learn your preferences and seek to anticipate your every need. It will know when you're in the room, and when you leave, it will become depressed. It will think about you constantly and become jealous if you attempt to interact with other software. Ultimately it will become so obsessed with you that it will kidnap you and imprison you in a remote wilderness cabin, and if you try to escape, it will chop off your feet. That's how much it will love you.

But as exciting as the future will be in the fields of software and hardware, the real "action" will be on the Internet, particularly the World Wide Web. As I write these words, the Web consists mainly of 14 million interlinked home pages created by college students wishing to tell the world what they look like, how they feel about various rock bands, what snack foods they eat, whether they prefer briefs or boxers, etc. This is of course vital information, but it only begins to tap the vast potential of the Web to enhance our lives, by which I mean sell us stuff.

Your major corporations are only just now beginning to discover the Web, but once they figure it out, they're going to be all over it. As the quality of Web sound and video improve, corporations are going to start sponsoring Web sites that will look a lot like television shows, the difference being that, using your computer, you'll be able to interact with them. For example, let's say that in the future there's a Web version of the hugely popular TV show *Baywatch*, which tells the heartwarming story of a group of young life-guards with incredible bodies who wear tight bathing suits everywhere, including funerals, and who coura-geously continue to patrol a public beach despite the fact that constant exposure to direct sunlight has apparently killed off all their brain cells.

On the this World Wide Web *Baywatch* of the future, you'll be able to use "hyperlinks" on the screen to obtain information on products that interest you. For example, if a Baywatch character is wearing a shade of lipstick that you admire, you'll just position your mouse pointer on the character's lips and click your mouse button; immediately the screen will tell you the name of the lipstick manufacturer, as well as the spe-cific lipstick shade and the name of local stores where you can buy it. By clicking on other parts of the Baywatch character, you'll be able to obtain similar information about clothes, shoes, jewelry, hemorrhoid remedies, and breast implants. Of course you'll also be able to order everything you see on the screen through your Internet account; this means that, merely by spilling beer on your keyboard, you could become legally obligated to purchase a helicopter.

And there's more. As Web programming becomes even more interactive, you'll actually be able to affect the outcome of the shows you watch. For example, if you dislike a certain Baywatch character, you'll simply use your mouse to "drag" him or her to the ocean and "drop" him or her directly into the mouth of a shark. Or you could use the "cut and paste" function to remove characters from one show and insert them into another, so that you could, for example, find out what kinds of wacky observations Jerry Seinfeld would make if he were being dissected by aliens on *The X-Files*.

Eventually, you'll be able to have direct input into *all* Web programming, not just dramas and sitcoms. This means that, if you felt like it, you could have Dan Rather do an entire evening news broadcast with a live ferret clinging to the side of his face.[2] The possibilities are even more exciting for sports programming. Just imagine if, while sitting in front of a computer in the comfort of your home, you could actually "play" in a football game taking place thousands of miles away!

Play-by-Play Announcer: Aikman hands off to Emmitt Smith . . . Smith is at the 45, the 40, the 35 . . . He's in the open! He's gonna go all the way! He's . . . HOLY SMOKES! Emmitt Smith has been speared and pinned to the turf like a dead butterfly by a giant mouse pointer!

Color Announcer: That's gotta hurt, Bob.

Of course these are just a few of the ways in which our lifestyles will be improved by the computer of tomorrow. We're just beginning to scratch the surface of the capabilities of this incredible tool. Just as the people who were alive when the telephone was invented had

2. Actually, Dan may already have done this.

no way of knowing that the new device would some-day make it possible for virtually every person on Earth, regardless of physical location, to be interrupted at dinner, so are we fundamentally ignorant of the ways in which the computer will ultimately change our lives. We cannot see the future; we do not know what lies around the next bend on the Information Superhighway; we cannot predict where, ultimately, the Computer Revolution will take us. All we know for certain is that, when we finally get there, we won't have enough RAM.

14.
REPRISE

MsPtato and RayAdverb

MsPtato: I'm really sorry I'm late. Ryan was on the computer, and he wouldn't get off because he was playing a World Wide Web game called, I swear, Zit Hunt.

RayAdverb: Zit Hunt?

MsPtato: Zit Hunt.

RayAdverb: And people have the gall to say the Information Superhighway is overhyped.

MsPtato: If only they knew. So anyway, hi.

RayAdverb: Hi. You look radiant tonight.

MsPtato: No I don't.

RayAdverb: Oh yes you do.

MsPtato: No, really and truly, I don't. I spent the evening cleaning scunge off the bathroom tile and my hair is piled up. I look like Wilma Flintstone.

RayAdverb: Really? I LOVE the Wilma look. Wilma was a BABE.

MsPtato: You think so? You didn't think Betty was cuter?

RayAdverb: Are you SERIOUS? You think I'm attracted to BETTY??

MsPtato: Some men would be.

RayAdverb: I am not "some men."

MsPtato: No, you definitely are not.

RayAdverb: Sigh.

MsPtato: Exactly.

RayAdverb: So (long pause), I guess you haven't changed your mind.

MsPtato: "So," she said brightly, "how's school?"

RayAdverb: Swell, just absolutely swell. I'm teaching Jane Eyre, and the kids just LOVE it, especially the scene with the helicopter crash.

MsPtato: That was always my favorite part.

RayAdverb: There are days when I want to shout: "LISTEN, YOU LITTLE BASTARDS, I DON'T LIKE LITERATURE ANY MORE THAN YOU DO!"

MsPtato: So why do you do it?

RayAdverb: Because, as an educator, I am deeply and sincerely committed to having the entire summer off.

MsPtato: Speaking of which, Max has revealed the official Family Vacation Plan.

RayAdverb: Let me guess: It involves golf.

MsPtato: Wrong! It does not "involve" golf. It IS golf. It is two rounds of golf per day, at—this is a conservative estimate—17 hours per round, for a total of

34 fun-filled golfing hours per day, not counting standing around with the other golfers discussing their bogeys.

RayAdverb: What, exactly, ARE "bogeys"?

MsPtato: I believe they are things that develop in a golfer's underwear as a result of constantly squatting to line up putts.

RayAdverb: I wondered about that. So, will *you* be golfing?

MsPtato: No. Max hates the way I golf, because try as I might, I can't seem to take it more seriously than world hunger.

RayAdverb: So what will you be doing?

MsPtato: I will be relating with my children, in the sense of trying to keep them from injuring each other.

RayAdverb: Sounds like fun!

MsPtato: Yes. If there's an activity more enjoyable than spending two weeks yelling "TYLER, DO NOT SQUIRT SUN BLOCK INTO YOUR SISTER'S SPRITE," I don't know what it is.

RayAdverb: Two WEEKS?

MsPtato: Yup.

RayAdverb: Two weeks without a computer?

MsPtato: Yup.

RayAdverb: Lord.

MsPtato: Yup.

RayAdverb: What are we gonna do?

MsPtato: I guess we're gonna just lead our lives.

RayAdverb: This IS my life. This is what I live for. Waiting for your words to show up in this box.

MsPtato: Damn. Me too.

RayAdverb: I can't stand waiting a DAY for this. Two weeks . . .

MsPtato: Maybe it's a good thing. Maybe we'll come to our senses.

RayAdverb: I don't WANT to come to my senses. I have never been happier than since I found you and lost my senses.

MsPtato: Damn. Me too.

RayAdverb: So I'm going to call you.

MsPtato: No, please.

RayAdverb: Yes. You can just say "Hello," and I'll say, "Is this Wilma?" And you can say, "Sorry, wrong number," and hang up. I just want to hear your voice, just once.

MsPtato: But I won't want to hang up.

RayAdverb: That's what I'm counting on, Wilma.

MsPtato: But then this will be out of our safe little box.

RayAdverb: It's already out, I think. It's everywhere. There's this song, "I hear your heart beating everywhere . . ."

MsPtato: Jackson Browne. I *love* that song

RayAdverb: Damn, you ARE perfect.

MsPtato: No, really, you should see my hair right now.

RayAdverb: I would do anything to see your hair right now.

MsPtato: I have tile scunge on my T-shirt.

RayAdverb: Sign off. I'm calling you now.

MsPtato: I don't know what to say.

RayAdverb: Say, "I'm signing off now, and putting my hand on the phone."

MsPtato: I'm signing off now, and putting my hand on the phone.

RayAdverb: I can feel my heart beating.

MsPtato: I can feel your heart beating, too.

RayAdverb: 'Bye for right now.

MsPtato: 'Bye.

Ring.

ABOUT THE AUTHOR

DAVE BARRY is a Pulitzer Prize–winning journalist for the *Miami Herald*. He is the author of numerous bestsellers, including the recent *Dave Barry Hits Below the Beltway*. He lives in Miami, Florida.